The New Pink Wine

The New Pink Wine
The New Pink Wine
The New Pink Wine
The New Pink Wine
The New Pink Wine

A Guide to the World's Best Rosés

Larry
& Ann Walker

BOARD AND BENCH
— PUBLISHING —
SAN FRANCISCO

The New Pink Wine:
A Guide to the World's Best Rosés

Copyright © 2018 Larry Walker

Wine Appreciation Guild
an imprint of
Board and Bench Publishing
www.boardandbench.com

No part of this publication may be reproduced, distributed,
or transmitted in any form or by any means, including
photocopying, recording, or other electronic or mechanical
methods, without the prior written permission of the publisher.

Editor: Judith Chien
Book Design: TIPS Technical Publishing, Inc.
Cover Design: Chris Matulich

Library of Congress Cataloging-in-Publication Data

Names: Walker, Larry, 1936- author. | Walker, Ann, 1944- author.

Title: The new pink wine : a guide to the world's
best rosés / Larry & Ann Walker.

Description: San Francisco : Board and Bench Publishing,
2018. | Includes bibliographical references and index.

Identifiers: LCCN 2018034367 (print) | LCCN 2018035049 (ebook) |
ISBN 9781935879053 (Epub) | ISBN 9781935879282 (alk. paper)

Subjects: LCSH: Rosé wines. | Cooking (Wine) |
Food and wine pairing. | LCGFT: Cookbooks.

Classification: LCC TP548.6.R67 (ebook) |
LCC TP548.6.R67 W35 2018 (print) | DDC 641.6/22--dc23

LC record available at https://lccn.loc.gov/2018034367

Although all reasonable care has been taken in the preparation
of this book, neither the author nor the publisher can
accept liability for any consequences arising from the
information contained herein or from use thereof.

Printed and bound in Canada

For all our friends and associates
who have helped Paint It Pink
for years and years.

CONTENTS

Contents

INTRODUCTION

STARTERS

*T*he food was good. The conversation was lively. The room was filled with laughter. There was a view of San Francisco Bay from the hillside Sausalito dining room, where a small group of professional women had come together for one of their occasional feasts.

The women wore pink. The tablecloth was pink. The wine in the glasses was pink. No special occasion. The group called itself the Pink Ladies and didn't need to have a special occasional to come together to drink pink wine and eat good food and have a good time.

As one said to the catering chef, "How could we not have fun when the wine is rosé? We are in the pink, for sure."

That pink dinner party was a good part of the inspiration for this book. But behind the fun and the laughter, there is a serious side to rosé. For too long, many wine drinkers have thought of rosé as a "beach wine," a "swimming pool wine," or a "summertime wine."

We believe this book will show that rosé is an "anytime" wine that can grace any meal, complementing a wide variety of food, as well as standing alone as a delicious apéro. Good rosé is a serious wine that has not forgotten how to giggle. You can invite it to a picnic in the park, a pool party, an afternoon at the beach, or uncork it for an evening of fine dining.

Welcome to the Pink World!

A PINK PRIMER

Part 1
Rosé in History

Upon her landing, Antony sent to her,
Invited her to supper. She replied
It should be better he became her guest;
Which she entreated. Our courteous Antony,
Whom ne'er the word of "No" woman heard speak,
Being barbered ten times o'er, goes to the feast.

—William Shakespeare, "Antony and Cleopatra"

Unfortunately, Shakespeare did not describe the feast enjoyed by Marc Antony and the Egyptian queen, neither the food nor the drink. There is a strong possibility that the wine Cleo and Antony shared was pink.

It isn't so much that Cleopatra thought, "I'll serve this swaggering Roman lout a nice pink wine, get him fuddled, have my way with him and save Egypt" (although that can't be ruled out). It's simply that most of the wines of the time were what we would call rosé.

This is because many of the winemaking techniques used to make today's darker, more tannic (and higher alcohol) red wines, such as extended maceration and mechanical pressing of the grapes, were not in the winemaker's playbook at the time. Grapes both red and white were hand or foot pressed very soon after harvest, extracting little tannin, so the juice was lightly colored. Even when more efficient wine presses were developed during Roman times, the resulting wine did not suit everyone's taste. According to contemporary reports, many wine drinkers found the more tannic wines harsh, and they were routinely cut with water. It is tempting to think of the deeply colored red wines of Anthony's time as something like the overly concentrated Cabernets of Napa Valley. But we won't go there for now.

It has been estimated that every citizen of Rome at the time of Antony drank about a liter of wine a day. How much of that was rosé we don't know. There was no A.C. Nielsen around to track market trends.

Where did all this wine come from? We know that in the early days of the Roman Republic, Greek wine was thought to be better and was more expensive than the local wines. But by the 2nd century BC Roman writers were aware that some vineyards produced superior wines, equivalent perhaps to what we call first growths or grand cru vineyards.

Bronze age amphora with Egyptian writing

The Romans were not the first to use the Mediterranean as a kind of wine superhighway. As early as 2500 BC the Egyptians shipped wine from the Nile Delta to many ports in the Middle East. And by 1500 BC the Phoenicians were shipping wine to southern France and Spain and, more to our point, planting vines there.

As the Roman Empire expanded, a booming wine trade developed with wine being shipped from Sicily, the coast of Spain and southern France. Wherever the Roman army went, the vine went with them. In developing and expanding the wine market, the Romans were doing what they did best: developing trade and commerce. Roman roads and bridges are still being used, as are the wine trade routes the Romans established.

The wines were shipped in amphorae, clay containers used for thousands of years around the Mediterranean, probably originating in Greece. Amphorae were made with a sharply pointed base that could be stuck into sand or dirt, then secured in racks to withstand transport by land or sea. They ranged from about one foot to five feet in height and held between 30 and 40 liters of wine. The amphorae were usually closed to oxygen with a float of olive oil or some other vegetable material. The Greeks often used rosin from conifers as a closure, which would account for the otherwise inexplicable Greek love of retsina, a wine flavored with rosin. These clay containers were also used in making wine, both for fermentation and for wine storage. Some modern winemakers are having another look at them, especially for the production of orange wine. More later.

The Phoenicians, with the help of Greek traders, played an especially key role in the history of pink wine. It is believed they were the first to develop vineyards around Marseilles and other parts of Provençe, a winegrowing region which could be called the modern motherland of rosé, because, as we have seen, much of the wine shipped around the Mediterranean was pink, and it has stayed pink right up until today.

As an example, the modern wine trade developed to a large extent on the wines of Bordeaux, which the English call claret, from a French word meaning lightly colored or clear. The most popular of the clarets was called *vin d'une nuit*, or "wine of one night," a very pale rosé left on the skins for a single night after harvest. Yorkville Cellars, a California winery, produces a rosé called Wine of One Night, which they translate rather loosely as

2017

YORKVILLE
CELLARS

VIN D'UNE NUIT
MADE WITH ORGANIC GRAPES
Rennie Vineyard

"wine of a one-night stand." (See Pink Choices, page 105.) Well, that works, too. Pink wines *are* more fun.

Part 2

How to Make a Pink Wine
(You could do it at home!)

There are three basic ways to make a pink wine, with some interesting variations. However, many rosé fanciers and dedicated rosé winemakers argue that there is only one "real" rosé. It's made by removing red wine from the skins and taking them to press after 24 hours or less of skin contact. That relatively limited skin contact limits the amount of color the proto wine absorbs, since wine color comes from the skin, not the flesh of the grape.

For red wine production, the grape juice might be left on the skin for up to a week or even longer. The longer it is left on the skins before pressing, the deeper color it will have. This period of skin contact is called maceration.

The limited time of maceration for rosé also impacts wine flavor and in most cases leads to a shorter shelf life. During maceration flavor compounds (phenolics and tannins) are absorbed. Without getting too technical, and speaking in general terms, because of short maceration time, rosé sometimes lacks the depth and intensity of flavor seen in red wines. Also, since there are elements in the grape skin that protect the wine from oxygen exposure, rosé tends to have a shorter shelf life than red wine or even white wine.

The mistaken opinion of many people who should know better is that rosé, lacking the tannic structure of red wine, is a lesser wine. Not true. Within that limited range, rosé flavors can be quite intense, quite satisfying. On the other hand, it does make most rosé easy to drink. Many consumers find this a plus, which may help explain the rapidly growing market for pink wine.

Vin gris, a delightful variation on basic rosé, is made by pressing red skin grapes immediately after harvest with no maceration. The name *vin gris* is a bit misleading. The wine is not, of course, gray but a very light pink.

Vin gris can be made from any red grape variety, although the light-skinned varieties, such as Gamay, Cinsault, and Grenache Gris are preferred, at least in France. One of the best pink wines from California is the Vin Gris de Cigare from Bonny Doon. It is an engaging and delicious blend of Grenache, Grenache blanc, Carignane, Mourvédre, Cinsault, and Rousanne.

Rosé can also be made by the *saignée* or "bleeding" technique. Early in the fermentation juice is removed from the must with the goal of producing a concentrated and deeply colored red wine. The rosé is almost an afterthought in this method as the "bled" juice may also be used to top up wine barrels or tanks or to produce a lighter red wine as a second label or cash flow

Vin Gris de Cigare Reserve aging in the cellar of Bonny Doon

wine. If the juice is removed early in the fermentation process it may be treated as rosé, although saignée is an unacceptable practice in regions where rosé is considered a serious wine. The Provençe Wine Council, for example dismisses such wines as not "true rosés." Perhaps not.

This purist approach is appealing, but it has one major fault: rosé made by the saignée method can be quite good. There are several examples in the Pink Choice section. Best to keep an open mind as well as an open palate.

There are two other ways to make a pink wine. It's best not to even think about them, but in the interest of completeness, we will have a quick look. First, a very modern approach is decolorization, which is not a word likely to be found in any paragraph discussing good rosé. Briefly, it involves using some form of charcoal to absorb the color compounds in the wine. Sounds like everyone's favorite: a charcoal infused glass of wine. Needless to say, the charcoal strips out a lot more than just color, but let's not get into that.

Finally, a rosé can easily be made by blending a red wine and a white wine. This method is illegal in most of France. At least there is no charcoal involved and the results can be tasty, but the purists insist that it isn't a "real rosé." These blends usually lack the fresh uplifted fruit flavors of a rosé made by the standard process. As noted, it is a rosé you could make at home if you wanted, impressing your friends with your Pink House Cuvée. Good luck with that.

However, the blending practice is quite common for sparkling wines and is allowed in the French region of Champagne.

There is one other category of wine which some are calling the "new rosé." It is called orange wine, and like the "old rosé" it is a very ancient style of winemaking, dating back thousands of years. It is a wine made from white grapes that are left to ferment on the skin, sometimes for several weeks, up to a year in some cases, so the production method is the opposite of rosé winemaking. These wines are not really orange, of course, but a dull pink, perhaps like a sunset seen through a haze of smog. Beyond that, orange wine is often fermented in the presence of oxygen in clay, sometimes made in the amphora shape, or in cement, which critics say can give the wine a flavor quite like flat beer. It is safe to say that orange wine is an acquired taste.

To be fair, orange wine has its fans, although it is a mystery why anyone would call it the "new rosé". The flavor profile is quite different since orange wine has only faded fruit flavors backed by bitter tannins.

Rosé is, of course, a pink wine, but there are many shades of pink. It is necessary to get a little technical in talking about the many shades of rosé, but let's try to keep it as simple as possible.

As mentioned above, the juice of almost all wine grapes is colorless. The color of red wine comes from phenolics in the grape skin called anthocyanins. Briefly and to cut short the lecture, these phenolics react with other elements in the wine—tannin being one of them—to produce color during the process of maceration as the wine ferments. There are other factors, but it is the length of maceration that largely determines the color of any given rosé wine.

The *Conseil Interprofessionnel des Vins de Provençe* has, with usual French bureaucratic thoroughness, created a chart identifying six colors: melon (cantaloupe), peach, red currant, grapefruit, mango, and mandarin.

There is some marketing evidence that consumers prefer the darker rosés. On the other hand, in tastings of rosé using black glasses to mask the color, tasters often opt for a lighter colored rosé. It is difficult to sort out the color preference question. There are certainly winemakers who make rosé for what they believe is consumer color preference, but in the end, the best rosé is likely to be based on what the grapes yield and how the wine tastes during production. The best rosé winemakers are perhaps colorblind.

Beyond the question of color, maceration time during fermentation also has an impact on flavor; the longer the maceration the more robust the flavor. Of course, the flavor is also affected by grape variety and *terroir.*

A word or two about terroir, one of the most misunderstood terms in the wine lover's vocabulary. Terroir includes far more than just the soil of the vineyard. It includes the local weather or microclimate of the vineyard; the angle of sunshine as it strikes the vine is especially important. In short, terroir is the total environment of the vine, from roots to grape. An expanded definition of terroir should include the human element, since that is part of the vine's environment, after all. It would also include how the vine is farmed and what the winemaker does in crafting the wine from harvest to wine in the bottle.

The base is, of course, the soil, the dirt where the vine grows. That is the bedrock of all wine, whether it be white, red, or pink. But the human element is important, too. Sometimes a young wine needs a nudge in the right direction. That's what winemakers are for.

What grape variety makes the best rosé? Truth is, there are excellent pink wines made from many different varieties. There are, however, at least four varieties that have consistently been part of the blend in outstanding rosé.

Cinsault, sometimes spelled Cinsaut, is an old variety, probably originally from southern France, where it is an important variety for rosé production in Provençe and Languedoc-Roussillon. It is considered a minor

Night harvest at Fiddlehead Cellars

variety in California, where it is used as a blending grape in Rhône varieties. Cinsault adds a spicy quality to rosé and an intense fruitiness.

Grenache (Garnacha in Spanish) adds a fullness and ripe fruit quality to rosé, especially when blended with Cinsault. Both varieties thrive in hot climates and are drought resistant as well. The variety originated in Aragon in northern Spain and was planted in Roussillon in southern France when Roussillon was part of the Kingdom of Aragon. The variety has several color variations, Grenache Gris and Grenache Blanc, which have become important in their own right. Grenache Noir, as the French call it, is an important component of red wine blends in the Rhône Valley and is the principal grape in the rosé wines of Tavel, Lirac, and Provençe. It is the dominant and sometimes the only variety in the excellent rosados from Rioja and other parts of northern Spain.

In California, Grenache was a mainstay of the cheap and cheerful jug wines of the Central Valley in the mid-20th century. It was little regarded as a variety on its own and was valued chiefly for high yields and high alcohol. It wasn't until the Rhône Rangers, that maverick group of California winemakers, who realized that the climate in much of the state was perfect for grape varietals grown in the Rhône Valley of France, hit the trail in the 1980s, that Grenache and other Rhône varietals became more important.

Syrah supplies key flavor elements in rosé—notably a spicy, fruity, mid-mouthfeel—and is widely used in the southern Rhône, Provençe, and Languedoc-Roussillon, where it adds to the body and rounded fruit flavors of the wines. Many winemakers believe that Syrah is especially responsive to terroir.

Another important grape for rosé is Mourvédre, as it is known in France. (In Spain, where the grape probably originated, it is called Mataro.) Wine made from Mourvédre can produce tannic wines of high alcohol, but properly treated the wine adds soft fruity, sometimes earthy flavors to rosé, especially in the Rhône Valley, Provençe, and Languedoc-Roussillon. It is a component of the rosé made in Jumilla in southeastern Spain, where it is called Monastrell.

As noted above, good rosé can be and is made from virtually any red-skinned wine grape. Gamay is an important grape in the production of *vin gris,* especially in the Loire Valley. Pinot Noir in particular makes excellent rosé and would probably be used more except for its great success as a red wine. In the Pink Choice section you will find rosé made from Amaral to Zinfandel, which covers the A-Z of rosé grapes. And should you be wondering, Amaral is a Portuguese red grape used in the production of Vinho Verde rosé.

Speaking of Zinfandel, let's deal with White Zinfandel or Blush Wines. The "Rush to Blush" was kicked off in the 1970s. Sutter Home winery in Napa made a respectable Zinfandel (the red one) using the saignée method, bleeding off a portion of the juice before fermentation

to increase the intensity of the red wine. This juice was then fermented to a dry wine, somewhat off-white, that the winery called White Zinfandel. All good so far.

The story goes that in 1975 the saignée juice did not ferment fully dry because of a stuck fermentation, that is the yeast died off before the grape sugars in the wine were completely converted to alcohol. The winemaker tasted the wine, which was still sweet of course, liked it, and shouted something like "Eureka," and it came to pass that White Zin was born.

Over the next few decades, White Zin sold about a zillion cases, satisfying the palate of those who like cold and sweet (think Coca-Cola) and infuriated wine snobs everywhere, who insisted that it wasn't "real wine" and certainly wasn't a "real rosé."

Regardless of the snob effect, White Zin is still selling very well—perhaps a gateway wine to dry rosé. There is no solid evidence for this, but sales of traditional dry rosé seemed to start trending when White Zin sales began to slacken.

So the next time you are enjoying a delicious glass of rosé, perhaps with a dozen raw oysters, give a nod to White Zinfandel, your auntie's pink wine. She made it all possible.

WHO IS DRINKING PINK?

The Nielsen Company, an organization that tracks sales of consumer products, has been keeping an eye on the increase in rosé sales. Danny Brager, senior vice president in the Beverage Alcohol division of Nielsen, confirmed that rosé sales are growing "extremely fast."

"The growth spurt started in 2012 and then exploded in 2013," he said. Growth is in the range of 40 percent annually.

Who is drinking all that lovely rosé?

According to Brager, rosé drinkers have an even higher income profile than most wine consumers, already a high income group.

"They are also ethnically diverse, more than the overall wine market, and skewed toward younger urban females," he said. Not surprisingly, the highest percentage growth in rosé sales are for wines priced at $20 and up.

Over half of all rosé sold in the US comes from France and about one-third from US producers.

PINK PROFILES

U.S.A.

*"Rosé Is Not Just
for Breakfast Anymore"*

—Kathy Joseph of Fiddlehead Cellars

California

Thank you, Kathy, for the perfect opening to the story of California rosé. She does have insider information since she makes one of the state's best at her Fiddlehead Cellars winery in Santa Barbara County.

What she was getting at is that it took California rosé a long time to grow up. Even before White Zinfandel, pink wine from the Golden State tended to be ponderous, flat, and sweet. It was almost always made from inferior grapes and often the result of faulty fermentation techniques. To be fair, following the repeal of prohibition in 1933, a lot of California red and white wine was also ponderous, flat, and sweet. Prohibition, which began in 1920, probably set California back 50 years, but that's another story.

An early example of a grown-up California rosé is Heitz Cellars Grignolino Rosé, which Joe Heitz made back in the 1960s. A few years later, Bob Mondavi released his Gamay Rosé, a pretty good wine, even if it wasn't Gamay, the famous red wine grape of Beaujolais. Robert wasn't trying to fool anyone. Most winemakers in California at the time didn't know that what they called Gamay was really an obscure southern French grape known as Valdiguie. Other early quality California pinks include

Caymus Oeil de Perdrix (eye of the partridge), Geyser Peak Rosé of Cabernet, David Bruce Pinot Noir Blanc, Mirassou Petite Rosé and Bonny Doon Vineyards Pinot Gris, made by Randall Grahm, the innovative winemaker and "president for life" of Bonny Doon Vineyards in the Santa Cruz Mountains south of San Francisco. Grahm was one of the principal players in the Rhône renaissance in California in the 1980s. His interest in grape varieties used in the Rhône Valley led him to rosé.

When asked why he decided to make pink wine, Grahm said, "Honestly, I don't precisely remember what motivated me to make pink wine in the first place, but it was not long before I realized that by bleeding our red grapes, we could concentrate the color of the remaining red must. We in fact began making *vin gris* in 1981 as a proper pink wine for a few years, then when we started with Cigare Volant, realized that we could chuck the saignée juice in with the lot, so we did."

When Grahm sold his mass-market Big House wine brand years ago he abandoned the saignée approach. "Since then, the wine has been made from bespoke grapes for the pink wine, i.e. no saignée, and we use essentially minimal skin contact. The grapes are harvested at an appropriate maturity level, typically about

21.5 Brix on average, so it is not necessary to manipulate the resultant alcohol," he said.

"We really try to eschew the quality of candied or artificial fruit in the young wine. As a result, we end up with a wine that is a lot more subtle and delicate than many pink wines. It tends to draw the consumer in rather than hit them over the head with a too aggressive aromatic profile. Normally, subtlety does not triumph in the marketplace, but we have been enormously lucky to find that in this case, it does," he added.

At present, the Bonny Doon Vin Gris is a blend of Grenache Noir, Grenache Blanc, Carignane, Mourvédre, Cinsault, and Rousanne. "I think that a blend is really the way to go. We are hoping, in fact, to design an extremely elegant, luxury cuvée of vin gris, which will be a blend of Tibouren, Mourvédre, Grenache Noir, Grenache Gris, and Clairette. We produced a Vin Gris Reserve in 2013, which was pretty cool indeed, a blend of Mourvédre, Grenache Noir, Cinsault, fermented in stainless but then aged in five gallon glass demijohns and bottled without filtration. Incredibly subtle with very great depth; I envision a new wine for us down the road that would build on this style."

There are those who say that pink wines cannot truly represent a sense of place or terroir, because of limited skin contact. Grahm, not surprisingly, disagrees. "Rosé can absolutely represent terroir, if the aromatic profile is not too exaggerated." He stipulated that the terroir factor in rosé was more likely from organically or biodynamically farmed grapes from a low-yielding vineyard.

Kathy Joseph, owner, winemaker, "chief grape herder and head fiddle" of Fiddlehead Cellars makes an outstanding rosé of Pinot Noir from Fiddlestix Vineyard in the Sta. Rita Hills American Viticultural Area in Santa Barbara County on California's Central Coast. It is a classic California coastal landscape with low rocky hills, broken by rugged canyons.

Kathy Joseph of Fiddlehead Cellars
in her Santa Barbara vineyard

It isn't that far from large population centers like Santa Barbara, and even Los Angeles is just over the hill and down the freeway, but there are pockets of wilderness where the occasional mountain lion can still be spotted. There are thousands of acres of vines and more than 50 wineries in the AVA, which is a cool climate region with coastal winds and fog which rolls up the east-west canyons from the nearby Pacific. Soils are marginal with high calcium content. It is best known for Pinot Noir and Chardonnay.

Joseph thinks it's a pretty good place to make rosé as well, and agrees with Grahm on the question of rosé and terroir. "The gorgeous black clay-loam soils of Fiddlestix allow me to showcase a lot of character with short skin contact time. So in my case, yes, a rosé can show the vineyard, but not everyone can do this, and even less so when the rosé is made by the saignée method," she said. "I pick specifically for the balance in the wine," she added.

Joseph said she believed the increased sales of pink wine owed a great deal to increased quality. "But I do credit and thank those early California rosés and producers for converting many customers to wine drinkers. Quite frankly, quality has improved and there are many more, very good, dry options with character out there to enjoy. And everyone has become way more experimental with when to drink rosés. They are not just for breakfast anymore!"

Joseph cited the soils of the Santa Rita Hills, but good rosé is made all over the state, except in the hot spots of the Central Valley, that ancient sea bottom that stretches hundreds of miles north from the Mexican border. Summer daytime temperatures often top 100°F in the Valley and it stays warm through the night. In general, wine grapes can take some heat during the day, but they like to cool down and slip on a cardigan after the sun goes down.

That combination of warm to hot days and cool nights fits much of coastal California, especially northern California, where Pacific fog may linger until noon in many vineyards near the sea.

There are two inland AVAs that also fit that pattern. The Sierra Foothills AVA is a wine grape-friendly area. It is one of the largest AVAs, stretching from north to south for about 200 miles along historic Highway 49. The landscape is rugged with deep canyons cut by streams that break up the land into jagged rockscapes. Soils are generally poor but certainly capable of supporting vines.

Grapes were first planted in Amador County during the California Gold Rush in the early 1850s. At the height of the Gold Rush there were dozens of small wineries in the region, producing wines for thirsty miners as well as for shipment down river to the boom city of San Francisco.

The best vineyards in the AVA are generally planted at between 1500 and 3000 feet in elevation, assuring cool evening breezes. There are about 6000 acres planted to grapes, with Zinfandel the most common, accounting for over 2000 acres.

There are over 100 wineries in the AVA, with a new one opening seemingly every day. Most are quite small, producing only a few thousand cases with a good many rosés in the mix.

One of the best is the Edmunds St. John Bone-Jolly Gamay Noir Rosé, made by Steve Edmunds. Edmunds has been making small batches of wine at his urban winery in Berkeley from a scattering of California vineyards for over 30 years. He has been known from the beginning as a "terroirist," someone who cares about the origin of the wines. He endorses the French saying, *la terre parle,* the earth speaks.

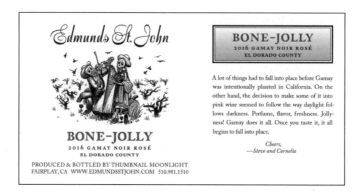

His Bone-Jolly Gamay Noir Rosé is the real thing. The grapes are from Witters Vineyard, planted in a volcanic clay-loam soil at an elevation of 3400 feet, one of the highest vineyards in the state. The site had been a pear orchard, but in 2000, as pear prices fell, it was planted to Gamay (the true Gamay not Valdigue), and Edmunds uses the grapes only for rosé. The wine is a light pink with fresh, juicy fruit, intense mouth feel and a long finish. (See Pink Choices, page 88)

Another rosé-friendly region is the Lodi AVA, which lies on the western edge of the Central Valley, about 100 miles east of San Francisco Bay in the delta region of the San Joaquin/Sacramento Rivers. As elsewhere in the Valley, days can get quite warm, but cool air off the Delta breezes in at sundown. The locals call it their "natural" air conditioning. The grapes like it, too.

Soils are alluvial with granite tones that add a depth and minerality to many Lodi wines. Known for old vine Zinfandels and Cabernet Sauvignon, Lodi has recently begun to show a little pink here and there. One of the best Lodi rosés is from Bokisch, a winery dedicated to Iberian varieties. The Bokisch Terra Ata Vineyard rosado is a blend of Garnacha and Barbera. The wine is loaded with luscious fruit but with good balancing acidity. Owner-winemaker Markus Bokisch credits the Barbera with adding complexity. (See Pink Choices, page 83)

There are, of course, many fine rosés from Napa and Sonoma, the North Coast counties that many think of as the heart of the state's premium wine territory, but the North Coast doesn't stop there as Donkey & Goat's Isabel's Cuvée shows. (See Pink Choices, page 88) Jared and Tracey Brandt started their winery, also in Berkeley, in 2004 after a trip to France convinced them they should make wine. A rosé from Mendocino County, up the road a piece from SoNap, was the first wine they released.

"The wine was released a few months after the birth of our first daughter, Isabel, so that was the name of the wine," Tracey Brandt said. "We had discovered this 1896 planting of Grenache Gris, and being fans of rosé, we jumped at the chance."

The Brandts are obviously happy with the vineyard, since they are still making a rosé from the century-plus vines. They believe that rosé can represent a vineyard as well as a red or white wine and the Isabel's Cuvée certainly makes that point.

"When the rosé starts in the vineyard, it absolutely can show the site. We only make rosé from those grapes. We pick for optimum acidity and flavor," she said. The wine is not fined or cleaned up by filtration or stabilization.

Tracey & Jared Brandt of Donkey & Goat Winery

"The wine ingredients are grapes and minimal SO_2," she said. This would also be a key in allowing the terroir, the vineyard itself, to show.

As for rosé and food, Tracey Brandt is true to her roots. "One that pops in my head is grilled shrimp and chorizo kebabs served over cheese grits. The grits are from North Carolina where I'm from, and my annual trip home includes replenishing my grits supply. The shrimp is marinated in an olive oil base with garlic, chili, and caraway seeds."

"I'm a year-round rosé drinker," she added.

Oregon

It's a well-worn story. In the mid-1960s three UC Davis students left the California wine scene behind and headed north for Oregon, where they believed they could make great Pinot Noir. David Lett, Charles Coury, and Dick Erath set up their winemaker tents in the Willamette Valley, a few miles from Portland, despite a warning from wine gurus that it was impossible to ripen wine grapes under the gray and gloomy sky of Oregon.

Now Oregon, and the Willamette Valley in particular, are recognized for world-class Pinot Noir. And, apparently while no one was looking, Oregon has also been turning out some very good rosé.

While the Willamette Valley AVA gets most of the attention, there is good potential for rosé in southern Oregon, an umbrella appellation containing several different AVAs. There is a history of grape growing in southern Oregon going back to the mid-19th century,

*David Lett christening the first planting of Vitis
vinifera (including Pinot Noir) in the Willamette Valley
in the spring of 1965 (Courtesy of Eyrie Vineyards)*

but it wasn't until 1961 that Hillcrest Vineyards, the first modern winery, was established in the Umpqua Valley, edging out Willamette by a few years.

Southern Oregon is somewhat warmer and drier than the north, which opens the potential for more varied styles of rosé.

However, Willamette Valle remains the most recognized AVA in Oregon and is also the largest, although it is now divided into six sub-appellations. There are over 500 wineries in the AVA, accounting for about 75 percent of Oregon's total wine production.

The AVA boundaries are based on the drainage basin of the Willamette River, running roughly north-south. The Cascade Mountains to the east block the most severe winter storms from the inland high plains, while gaps in the coastal mountains to the west allow cool Pacific winds to break through in the summer.

Valley soils are principally volcanic and sedimentary seabed, often buried beneath gravel, rock, and boulders from ancient flooding. Summers are dry and warm, but temperatures seldom climb above 90°F and very rarely drop to 0°F. There are fairly heavy rains in winter and early spring, but little snow.

Good weather for grapes.

FRANCE

Rosé is made, and drunk, wherever grapes grow in France. Walk into a humble café in the smallest village or a grand café in Paris and there is sure to be a house rosé on offer. And you can be sure it will be ordered often throughout the day.

There is good rosé everywhere in France; however a book covering the whole of Pink France would be far more work than we are inclined to undertake. Also, much of it is consumed locally and is never found outside the region. This book is focused on the major rosé zones, beginning with Provence, where the story of French rosé begins.

Provence

It was near the end of a long road trip, Paris to the Mediterranean and back again. We had no itinerary, no reservations, no goals. We barely took notes, consulted no guidebooks beyond a battered copy of *Adventures on the Wine Route* by Kermit Lynch, the Berkeley wine retailer and importer who has been responsible for turning a lot of people on to rosé.

We had gone as far south as Les-Saintes-Maries-de-la-Mer in the heart of the Camargue, that sprawling marshy plain where the Rhône meets the Mediterranean. A remarkable landscape, far removed from the typical food and travel magazine Provençal photo layouts of lavender fields and miles of vineyards. Modern travelers go the Camargue to birdwatch—there are over 400 species of birds there—or to snap photos of horsemen, often riding through water up to the stirrups, tending herds of horses and cattle, including the fighting bulls used in the Provençal bullfights. In the Camargue version, the corrida is bloodless, for the bull at least. The torero, who is unarmed, must pluck a flower from the bull's horns while avoiding death himself. Let's hope he gets a glass of rosé to steady his hand.

Saintes-Maries has been a pilgrimage site for centuries. Legend has it that in AD 40 Mary, the mother of Jesus, Mary Salome, the mother of James and John, Mary Magdalene, Martha and her brother Lazarus, and their servant Sarah, were cast out to sea in a small boat. With divine guidance, the boat came safely ashore near where an ancient church now stands. The various Marys and Sarah remained in Camargue, where they were buried. Their grave is now a shrine which has been a pilgrimage site for gypsies for centuries—the gypsies having some sympathy for refugees cast up on a strange shore.

*View Of Aiguines Village Overlooking Lac de Sainte
Croix Lake-Alpes de Haute Provence, France*

We visited the shrine on a drizzly April afternoon, the kind of day when the sea and the land seemed to merge and mingle, a misty canvas of pale shades of gray, like a Turner painting.

We arrived in Arles, a few miles inland, later in the afternoon. We were lucky to find a room in Le Relais de Poste, a comfortable mid-range hotel near the town center, a short walk from the Espace Van Gogh, which must be the world's only tourist site based on the loss of an ear. The original building, dating from the 16th century, was a hospital. Van Gogh was committed there after he cut off his left earlobe in 1888.

The space in front of the former hospital has been planted to resemble his painting, Le Jardin de l'Hotel de Dieu. The Arles library is now housed there as well as several well stocked souvenir shops—postcards, anyone?—and a café.

Like good tourists we bought postcards—sunflower, anyone?—had a pastis in the café and started to think about dinner. Where? Back out on the street, postcards written and addressed but not yet mailed, we checked out nearby restaurants. A few were tempting, but not what we wanted. We were looking for something basic, something simple. And we found it. It was a charcuterie with a few tables and a takeout counter where we filled a small bag with various bit of dried pig for a picnic in our hotel room. The wine was from the hotel restaurant. Rosé, of course. We are in Provence. Two bottles, *s'il vous plait.*

***

Rosé is a very big deal in Provence. Just how much of it is consumed during hotel room picnics is not clear, but exports of Provençal pink to the US have been growing in double digits for the past several years.

Over half of all wine produced in Provence is rosé, with the large Cotes de Provence AOC, between Nice and Marseille, responsible for about 80 percent of total rosé production in Provence. Grenache is the dominant grape in Cotes de Provence. The Coteaux d'Aix-en-Provence AOC, in the western part of Provence, is the second largest, with Grenache and Mourvédre dominating. In the Bandol AOC in southwestern Provence Mourvédre is the most important grape, with about one-third of total production being rosé.

Sacha Lichine is partly responsible for the surge of rosé sales in the US, although by the standards of Provence where rosé has been made for several thousand years, he is a newcomer. Lichine began making wine in the Cotes de Provence in 2008, having sold Château Prieuré-Lichine, the Fourth Growth Bordeaux estate that he inherited from his father, the wine writer and merchant Alexis Lichine.

Asked what makes the quality of Provençal rosé stand out, Lichine pointed to a "convergence of factors" including a temperate climate year around. "The predominant grape variety of Côtes de Provence is Grenache, which gives the rosé produced in this region body and fruit."

Speaking of his own wines from Château d'Esclans—
Rock Angel, Les Clans and Garrus (see Pink Choices,
page 112)— Lichine said the wines showed "complexity and structure in addition to unusual length." He
noted that the two high-end wines, Les Clans and Garrus, are fermented in oak, unusual for a rosé. "Terroir
plays an important role, as it is at the root of producing quality fruit; the wine making process is of equal
importance and therefore needs to match everything
that leads up to it," he added.

"In the case of Garrus, the Grenache grapes that are used to make it come from a single vineyard with vines from 70–100 years in age, growing on hilly slopes that are rich in limestone," he said. "The vines are situated on an elevated plateau with a unique microclimate. This contributes tremendously to giving Garrus a remarkable standout quality relative to the other wines produced at Château d'Esclans," he added, with a nod toward terroir.

Lichine, like thoughtful winemakers everywhere, was talking about wines reflecting their origin, the soils that nourished the roots that feed the grapes. He was talking about the spirit of the land.

You are on the open Mediterranean here so the waves are breaking closer to shore and there is a downward chop, different from the gentle surf in Collioure. We settled into our chairs, perhaps 100 yards up from the surf break, a bowl of olives and a bottle of rosé on the table beside us. The rosé, a 100 percent Grenache, was from L'Avail Winery, one of our neighbors in the Agly Valley, west of Perpignan. The olives were from a grove in the Corbières Mountains, a few miles inland. Eating and drinking locally is not a trendy food movement in Roussillon. It's just the way things are.

After we had spent a few hours soaking up the sun, the olives were gone and the bottle was empty. It was time, we decided, for some serious eating, which meant oysters from the local lagoon. A few miles outside the village a small spit of sand backed up to the Etang de Leucate, separated from the Mediterranean by a narrow dune. The area is called Grau de Leucate, *grau* in the ancient Occitan language meaning a small opening from an *etang*.

There is a row of shacks fronting a gravel road and dirt parking area. The shacks, seen from a distance, look abandoned, derelict, hammered almost constantly by a brisk wind blowing in from the sea. This is a very different postcard from the one found in Collioure. Up close, the "shacks" turn out to be restaurants and a few retail markets selling oysters, mussels and fish fresh from the lagoon.

By sunrise small boats are unloading the harvest from the lagoon onto docks at the rear of the row of restaurants and shops, having come from the lagoon via a series of narrow canals. The oysters and mussels are farmed and are a variety found only on the southeastern coast of France and further south on the Mediterranean coast of Catalonia.

Our favorite is the family-owned L'Aquirum. Like the other restaurants in this oyster-farming center, L'Aquirum has its own boat to harvest the oysters, mussels, sea snails and the other juicy treats from the water.

The oysters come in several different sizes. We prefer the smaller ones and have no problems downing a couple of dozen each. The oysters really don't need any accompaniment, other than perhaps a few drops of lemon juice, and naturally, a bottle or two of rosé from the Leucate Cooperative Winery, punctuated with an occasional bottle of Picpoul, a superb and supple white wine from the nearby Picpoul AOC. The wine is made from a grape of the same name.

We asked our waitress, a charming young woman with, inexplicably, a tattoo of Santa Muerte, the Mexican goddess of death on her arm, what the name of the grapes in the rosé was.

She said she would ask her mother who was working inside. She returned quickly, and without a hint of a smile, said, "She calls them Pierre or Sylvie because she can never remember all their names."

NAMING THE GRAPES

Collioure is everyone's dream of a French village on the Mediterranean. Find a table in the sun at any of the dozens of waterfront restaurants, order fish that most likely was swimming in the nearby sea less than 24 hours before, sip a glass of rosé that was made at a winery a short walk away from grapes grown on a nearby terraced hillside that you can see from your chair. Collioure is life on a postcard. And nothing wrong with that. Postcards can be fun and everyone likes to get a postcard now and then.

But if you want to put the postcard aside, drive an hour or so north along the coast and you will come to a region of beaches and small inlets or lagoons called étang in French. These lagoons are shallow with narrow openings into the sea spreading south from the village of Leucate. There is an outstanding beach in the village itself, further enhanced by the usual French beach amenities such as comfortable chairs, umbrellas and a generous supply of food and drink from the beachside bar.

Roussillon

Roussillon in southeastern France is one of the world's oldest wine growing regions. Vineyards were established there by Greek traders as early as the 7th century BC, more than 2700 years ago. Yet very few wine drinkers today have ever heard of Roussillon.

That hasn't always been the case. During the rise and expansion of the Roman Empire, wines from Roussillon and nearby vineyards dominated the Mediterranean wine trade. This continued into the Middle Ages, when the trade in Roussillon wines turned toward northern France and Flanders. In the 17th century the opening of the Midi Canal linked the Mediterranean with the Atlantic, and Roussillon wines traveled by river barge to the west coast of France and across the channel to England.

However, as the wine trade became more global and wine consumers had more choices, Roussillon wines began to lose favor to other regions. By the 20th century, the Roussillon was known as a supplier of cheap wines of doubtful quality or as a source of sweet wines.

Today, that story is changing. Young winemakers who are passionate about their wines are coming to Roussillon from other parts of France as the word has spread that not only can vineyards be bought for a bargain, compared to regions like Bordeaux or Burgundy, but that the vineyards have a strong story to tell. It isn't just about the money. Once more wines from Roussillon and Languedoc are being recognized for their quality. That includes rosé, although much of it is drunk close to home.

Among the new wave of winemakers is Caroline Bonville. She came to Roussillon from Bordeaux, where her father was the winemaker at Château Marac in the Entre-Deux Mers. Caroline's first job was as assistant to the cellar master at Château Figeac in St. Emillion. After some time in South Africa she established Mas Karolina in 2003 in Maury, a small wine village at the foot of the Pyrenees about an hour's drive from Spain.

What was she looking for in Roussillon?

"It starts with the soil. My vineyard is planted on perhaps the finest bedrock in France—granite and schist," she said.

Most of us know what granite is, but what is schist and why should it be a good bedrock for grape vines? In appearance, schist (and shale) form large flat stones, rather soft. These stones retain moisture, and they also release minerals into the soil, which could be reflected in the intensity of the wine. Other parts of the wine world where schist is considered an ideal vineyard component are the Priorat in Spain, the Douro Valley in Portugal, and the Mosel Valley in Germany.

Bonville's vineyard also contained a small plot of old vine Cinsault, which she knew was a key element in the great rosé wines of Provence. "The Cinsault adds more mineral flavors to the wine, balances the aromatics of Syrah and Grenache," she said.

"My aim is to produce a rosé that we can drink both before dinner and during dinner. What I'm looking for

Ripe Cinsault

in a rosé is a roundness in the mouth with good minerality and fruit tones," Bonville added.

She said that people often think of wines from the Roussillon as concentrated high alcohol red wine, but "that is beginning to change. People are finding rosé from Roussillon quite attractive."

Agreed. Rosé from Roussillon and Languedoc are stepping up to challenge Provence as the rosé center of the universe.

WORKING THE VINES

I met Caroline Bonville on a pleasantly warm June morning in the small plaza in front of the Mairie. It was the first time I had been there so early in the day and I was surprised at the activity. It was bustling, or about as bustling as the village of Maury ever gets. There was a steady flow in and out of the village's only bakery at the edge of the square. There was a stir of life around the mayor's office and Thierry, the greengrocer, and other vendors were setting up for the small market day, off-loading produce, cheese, and other goods from vans onto display tables.

Caroline arrived promptly and I climbed into her Citroën. We drove out of town, heading south across Le Maury, a small stream cutting through the middle of the village, which feeds

(continued)

into the Agly River a few miles to the east. We drove up the road about halfway to Lesquerde, another wine village which, like Maury, had its own co-op winery. We were headed for a small plot of Syrah to work on trellising the youthful vines.

Bonville talked about coming to Maury in the early 2000s, considering it a good location for farming vines organically. She said that she now owns a half dozen small vineyards, from two to four hectares—and is building a tasting room in the nearby town of Saint Paul de Fenouillet. She admitted that it was hard to balance her life as a hands-on vineyard worker/manager, winemaker, and single mother, but she is intent on promoting the wines of Roussillon and helping to improve the region's growing reputation for quality wines.

She credited her vineyard crew, which was mostly from an old Maury winemaking family, with helping her settle in as an outsider and a woman making wine on her own, not an easy thing to do in a rural French village.

We worked steadily, Bonville as hard as anyone. As the sun climbed the sky and warmed the vineyard and surrounding countryside, the smells of garrigue filled the air. I breathed in the heavily scented air and was transported back to the dinner the night before on the terrace of the village house where I was staying. She had brought her wines to the dinner of grilled lamb, fresh salad, and a squash terrine, and the memory of the scent of herbs from the dinner and the intense smell of the garrigue around the vineyard seemed to blend into the sensory memory of her Mas Karolina wines.

As we worked side by side Bonville talked more about her plans. She is confident about her wines and sells all she produces. She is adamant about keeping production low and always working toward improving quality.

Midway through the morning we took a break in the shade of a *cassot*, the local Catalan name for the small stone houses that were erected in vineyards, originally for the storage of vineyard tools and even for overnight sleeping quarters for vineyard workers in the days before the automobile.

Having worked in vineyards in Spain, just across the border, when I was a student there, I was expecting a cup of local red wine with some bread, cheese, and maybe a local sausage.

Wrong. Once again, France is not Spain and certainly not the Spain of my youth. We ate chocolate and drank bottled water while the vineyard crew grilled me on geopolitics and why Yankee Americans are afraid to travel in France. I informed them there were certainly many dangers in France, even locally. You never know what can happen when enjoying oysters in Leucate on the shore of the Mediterranean or grilling and sipping wine on the terrace at our village house or—even, heaven forbid—trellising vine shoots with the crew from Mas Karolina. They agreed and told me I was very brave.

(continued)

Shortly after noon, as the sun rose higher and hotter above the hillside, Caroline called it a day. We were just in time to get back to the village for lunch at the local bar, La Placette, and a bottle of Mas Karolina rosé. We had once again avoided the dangers of the French countryside.

—David Walker
(David Walker is a cultural geographer with a particular interest in the geography of wine.)

Tavel

Tavel is the only wine AOC in France where only rosé is produced. A bit strange, considering that Tavel is in the southern Rhône Valley, an area dominated by red wines, and just across the Rhône River from Châteauneuf-du-Pape, famed for its red wines.

As in much of southeastern France, Grenache is the chief grape of Tavel rosé, with a minimum of 60 percent of the blend, with Cinsault, Syrah, Carignane and sometimes Picpoul making up the rest, with an occasional dash of more obscure regional varieties.

It is possible that Tavel rosé gets its intensity from the method of fermentation. Whole clusters of red and white grapes are dumped into the crush tank and the grapes are pressed by their own weight, with the juice seeping through to the bottom of the tank. This free-run juice is then drained off and the wine fermented. This creates a more robust rosé with richer, more rounded fruit. Tavel rosé is that rare rosé that improves with aging, gaining a roundness seldom found in a rosé.

OTHER FRENCH PINKS

Alsace

There is very little rosé made in this northern region. Over 90 percent of the wine is white, chiefly from Riesling and Gewürztraminer, varieties that are not much used in rosé. However, don't pass up a chance to have a glass of Crémant de Alsace rosé if offered. (Crémant is a sparkling wine made just as champagne is made but with less atmospheric pressure in the bottle, which subdues the bubble action a bit.)

Crémant is made all over France but about half of total production is from Alsace. Only Pinot Noir is used in making Crémant rosé from Alsace, and it is an inexpensive alternative to Champagne but it has much more going for it that good value. At its best, the wine is supple with an elegant restrained fruit and a refreshing acidity. (See Pink Choices, page 74)

Chattillon sur Marne, Champagne region.

Champagne

Defining a rosé from the Champagne region gets a bit tricky. There is, first of all, a wide color variation ranging from a bright pink to the hue of copper you might see on a penny coin.

There is also the category called *blanc de noirs*, or a white wine made from red grapes. These are basically white sparklers with just a pale shade of pink. Roughly 5 percent of annual champagne production is rosé, excluding the blanc de noirs.

The prominent statue in the foreground is that of Pope Urban II.

Only three grapes are permitted in the production of champagne, the white grape Chardonnay and two red grapes, Pinot Meunier and Pinot Noir.

Champagne is also the only region in France where rosé can be made by blending a bit of red wine into a white wine. This is a strict no-no in other areas, like Provence. This method can actually add a depth and fullness to the champagne.

Loire Valley

Rosé is an important wine in Loire. There is a light drink-me-now style known as Rosé d'Anjou, which often has a sweet finish. A rather more serious rosé is Cabernet d'Anjou, made from Cabernet Franc and Cabernet Sauvignon. It is usually dry with a firm acidity. This style of Loire pink can age for a few years and becomes more rounded and firm.

A much larger appellation, Rosé de Loire is a bit of a compromise between the two but is usually made in a fruity style with light cherry fruit.

THE IBERIAN PENINSULA

Spain

Rosé in Spain and Portugal is called rosado and is produced in great quantity and often with high quality. In Spain, the most important wine grape for rosado is Grenache, or Garnacha as it is known in Spain. Other grape varieties important in rosé production are Tempranillo, Carignane, and Graciano.

Like rosé in France, rosado is found everywhere in Spain, with some of the recent best made in Rioja. Mention wine from Rioja and most wine drinkers think red. Javier Murua, co-owner of Bodegas Muriel says they should think again. "There is a long and deep tradition of rosados here in Rioja," he said. "Historically, rosado-type wines, often known as 'clarets' were the most important wines up until the mid-19th century."

Asked what taste profile he was looking for in the excellent Bodegas Muriel Rosato (see Pink Choices, page 127), he said "The main aim is to reflect the fruit. Our rosados, like most Mediterranean rosés, are meant to be consumed within a year of the vintage, so the important thing is to express a fruity freshness rather than acidity. In making the rosado, we are looking for a fresh, informal and easy-to-drink wine."

However, he noted, there was a certain amount of natural acidity that came from the main Rioja red grapes, Tempranillo and Garnacha. As for the question of rosé expressing a particular terroir, Murua said, "It does somewhat, although not as much as red or white wine. Our rosados represent terroir in a quite general sense, that of a region that balances the Mediterranean and Atlantic climates."

He added, "They also bear a slight reflection of the ecosystem of this land, made up of Mediterranean aromatic forest, rosemary, thyme, and wild blackberries."

Murua agreed that rosado was a versatile food wine, matching with many different dishes. "Any summer meal, especially rice dishes like paella or risottos. In Spain we serve melon with ham, a dish that matches wonderfully with rosado," he said. "But rosado is an any-season wine. It goes well with tomato-sauced pasta, for instance. And it is perfect with pizza."

Pizza and pink wine. That sounds just fine.

***

Bodegas Torres, one of the best-known wineries in Spain makes three rosados, two in Spain and one in Chile, which adds an international accent to the Torres family of pink wines. Miguel A. Torres, who is president of Torres, said that the Spanish rosados and the

Chilean pink obviously have very different flavor profiles as they are made from different grape varieties. "However," he added, "vinification is similar, as both ferment at low temperatures with very short skin contact."

Josep Sabarich, the chief winemaker of Bodegas Torres in Spain, agreed. "Indeed both styles of rosés have their own typicity. In Spain mostly Garnacha and Tempranillo are used for making rosés, whereas in Chile the more typical varieties are Cabernet Sauvignon, Merlot, and Syrah. Garnacha in modern rosés brings floral, citric, and orange notes to the wine. Tempranillo brings red fruit like strawberries and cherries. With the varieties used in Chile, the rosés will have more flavors of blackcurrant and blackberries with green notes of paprika and pepper in the background."

Sabarich noted that the style of rosé had changed in the past twenty to thirty years. "Today the Spanish rosés have stepped out of the shadow of the traditional white- and red-wine categories and have developed into a more premium wine with more subtle, perfumed, and especially floral notes."

Beyond the flavor profile added by the grape variety, Sabarich believes that a rosé can represent terroir as well as a red or white wine, if the grapes are properly farmed. "As I mentioned, there is a trend for rosés with more personality and complexity, and to achieve that you have to start in the vineyard," he said.

Torres' rosés are made from grapes grown in rosé-specific vineyards farmed to have a different aroma composition and different harvest times. "We harvest earlier to have more acidity in our rosé," he said, citing one example of how growing vines for rosés differs from growing grapes for red or white wines.

Torres is justly proud that their Santa Digna rosé from Chile (see Pink Choices, page 134) and their Chilean rosé sparkling wine, Estelado, are certified as Fair Trade wines. These are wines that are produced by workers paid a living wage in safe working environments. Grapes used in Fair Trade wines are grown without the use of pesticides.

Torres is also seeing a positive reception from consumers for higher quality rosé. As a result, the bodega is developing more premium rosados to add to their portfolio. According to Sabarich, restaurants are especially enthusiastic. "We have an outstanding price to quality ratio," he said.

What about rosé and food?

The Torres family has a long-standing interest in matching food and wines. The winery sponsors a conference every two years in Barcelona called the Wine & Culinary Forum, where leading chefs and sommeliers from around the world meet to discuss the relationship and interaction between food and wine.

Miguel A. Torres pointed to a classic food-rosé pairing. "When, for example, we have paella for lunch, we often have it with a rosado, which is a great match."

Indeed, there are few things that sharpen the appetite on a warm summer day like the sight of a paella on the table and a couple of bottles of chilled rosado.

***

EAT AND DRINK LOCALLY

There were 14 of us seated around a long table in a cellar room of La Casa del Conill, House of the Rabbit, in the small village of Sant Miquel d'Olèrdola, about an hour's drive from Barcelona in the heart of Catalonia. The restaurant, founded in 1812, is in a sprawling old mas or country house, divided into several rooms. We learned that the cellar is where they seat groups that they

(continued)

judge will need frequent wine refills, so that the waiters will not have to carry the wine upstairs.

Although we were only a few miles from the ramblas in Barcelona, surely one of the most esoteric if not downright weird cityscapes anywhere in the world, at the Casa Conill we were deep in the Catalan countryside. This was where the mystic Catalan spirit and the very practical Catalan ego hang out together. (See almost anything by Gaudi.) The nearest town of any size is Vilafranca del Penedés, the most important winegrowing center in Catalonia. Think of Napa without the t-shirts, cute little B&Bs, and pricey shops. Just miles and miles of vineyards and working bodegas. And a sprinkling of restaurants that will keep you eating until way past midnight.

We were a mixed medley of humans come together to celebrate several birthdays, wedding anniversaries and life in general.

Two friends from California had rented a house in the nearby beach town of Sitges and had the happy thought of bringing us all together.

A lunch had been arranged at the Rabbit's House. We sat down at 2 pm and didn't finish the last course and the last glass of wine until after 6 pm. The food, rich and satisfying Catalan country fare—including rabbit in garlic sauce—was abundant, as was the wine. Speeches were made, toasts were given and received. Plans for future reunions were plotted.

Someone counted the empty wine bottles on a corner serving table. No, I won't tell you how many there were but I will say that over half had contained rosado. A member of the group, who was a geographer and so was interested in such things, asked one of the waiters where the rosado was from.

"Ah, you liked it?"

"Yes. Very much. It went well with the food. Had good acidity and a long finish. It might be interesting to visit the vineyard."

"You won't have far to go, señor. The wine is from a vineyard 200 meters up the road."

That's about as local as you can get.

Portugal

California winemaker Randal Grahm once described Portugal as a "living museum of wine grapes." Vines are grown in every part of the country, and many of the vines, first brought by the Phoenicians and later the Romans, are not found elsewhere and are not well known outside of Portugal.

The coast of Oporto circa 1540

Rosé is, of course, made everywhere in Portugal, but some of the best of the new rosés are from the Vinho Verde region in the north, one of the oldest wine areas in the country. The Romans, who knew a bit about wine, imported wine from Vinho Verde. In modern times, the region became known for white wines, but rosé is gaining in importance and in quality.

Most Vinho Verde, whether pink, white or red, has a slight fizz and can sometimes finish with a spoonful of sugar. If you are not a fan of sweet and fizzy, it is important to taste a lot of Vinho Verde to be sure you are getting the right one for your palate. On the other hand, you could step out of your "no sweet wine" box and learn to appreciate this traditional approach to wine. "Love the one you're with" is a key message in wines as well as human relations.

The chief grapes used in rosé are Vinhao, Azal Tinto, and Espadeiro. They have in common a peppery fruit profile with sometimes a touch of chocolate. The Vinhao has an intensity of color that adds a deep pink to the color profile of many rosés.

Vinho Verde translates literally as "green wine," but it more properly means a "young wine" or "spring wine" since most Vinho Verde is sold in the spring following the harvest of the previous year.

Traditionally, grapes in the region were often trained to grow on a high trellis or pergola, with vegetables planted underneath the vines. Most of those traditional vineyards are gone, but on some of the back roads south of the Minho River, which forms the border between Portugal and Spain, some of the old plantings can still be spotted, scattered among stands of pine forests and Eucalyptus, very reminiscent of the Northern California coast. If you are particularly lucky you may even find a farmstead winery, producing traditional low-alcohol Vinho Verde.

Travel Alert: If you follow the highway north from Valenca do Minho and cross the Spanish border you will be in Galicia on the ancient pilgrim route, the Camino de Santiago. If you follow in the footsteps of the pilgrims of the Middle Ages you will find wines very similar to Vinho Verde, especially Albriño.

Try one for the road.

***

Bartholomew Broadbent imports and represents wines from all over the globe, including several rosés. "I do love rosé," he said. "And there is a growing market for rosé, but we have a long way to go to match the French, who for several years have been drinking more rosé than white wine."

He said he was pleased by the marketing success of the Broadbent Vinho Verde rosé. (See Pink Choices, page 123) "We had expected it to be about 10 percent of the sales of our Vinho Verde white but it is about 25 percent of white sales. Our single biggest selling wine in our portfolio is the Broadbent Vinho Verde. Our number three selling wine is the Broadbent Vinho Verde rosé."

Broadbent said that the rosés in his portfolio sell well year around, yet retailers and wholesalers cut rosé selections during the fall and winter. "It is frustrating. If they would only keep the rosé offerings, they would see that sales would continue, to some worthwhile extent, during the winter months."

And who is drinking all that rosé?

BROADBENT

VINHO VERDE ROSE

DENOMINAÇÃO DE ORIGEM CONTROLADA

Product of Portugal

"I would say that, in America, it is still predominantly women who buy rosé, but that is changing. I think it is beginning to reach the main stream American wine market. Unfortunately, too many people think that France makes the best rosé. This is like saying France makes the best red wines. It is nonsense. Great red, great white, and great rosé is made on every continent where wine is made. In fact, I would say that France makes the simplest rosés. For great rosés, I'd recommend people look to places like South Africa."

Broadbent may lose a few friends in France with that remark.

OTHER PINKS

Surprising South Africa

While we were researching rosé for this book—and, yes, that meant tasting a lot of wine—someone asked if there were any surprises. A lot of surprises, actually, but one that stands out is the high quality of South African rosé. There are not a lot of them in the Pink Choices, simply because not a lot of South African wine is available in US markets. I suspect there will be much more South African rosé available in the next few years.

The first vineyards in South Africa were planted in 1655, but not a lot of rosé was made for several centuries. However, domestic consumption of rosé is on a steady upward trend, almost doubling since 2009.

Is there an identifiable style of South African rosé? Not really.

Charl Coetzee, the winemaker at Babylonstoren (see Pink Choices, page 131) said, "There are so many ways to make a rosé that, except for the rosé of Provence, there is not really a "typical rosé." He said that for his winery, he was happy with a rosé based on Mourvédre. "Demand is so high that we have to buy in Mourvédre from different regions to make enough to supply the market."

Adam Mason of Mulderbosch winery (see Pink Choices, page 133) agreed that it was better for a winery to "carve out a unique style rather than a regional style." Mulderbosch rosé is based on Cabernet Sauvignon, which is not typical of South Africa, or anywhere else for that matter.

Mason said that in making a rosé he looked for freshness and elegance. "I want delicate perfume, lighter alcohol. For many, rosé tends to be an apéritif or a lighter style quaffing wine, so it should be something that presents a lighter, more delicate personality than more full-bodied wines."

Coetzee said that color was the first thing that attracted his attention. "I would definitely look for a rosé with a lighter, salmon color. Then I look for the dry, crisp style," he said. "I want to believe there are a few producers here in South Africa who have really put time and effort into rosé. I think, at the moment, rosé is the 'in' thing."

Italy

For many US wine drinkers, rosado from Italy can be summed up as: "Riunite on ice. That's nice." Yes, that's the punch line of TV commercial that helped drive sales of millions of cases of pink wine in the 1970s. For several years it was the top selling imported wine in the US. It was available in red, white and rosé, but check out the commercials on YouTube. The sweet pink stands out.

The wine is made from Lambrusco, an ancient grape variety. The Etruscans and Romans made wine from Lambrusco, and it is quite possible that it was sweet and pink. It's a pity that most wine drinkers know Lambrusco only as a sweet wine. It makes a good dry wine as well, with an intriguing bitterness on the finish. There are over 60 clonal variations of Lambrusco found throughout Italy, including Sicily, although only a handful are common.

Like the Vinho Verde region of Portugal, Lambrusco grapes historically were trained on a high trellis or pergola system and even trained to climb trees.

There are also good pink sparkling wines (see Pink Choices, page 76), but rosé made from the Sangiovese grape is usually the top choice. The wine typically opens on a strawberry note with good acidity. The best are reminiscent of a light-bodied Chianti.

Generally speaking, rosé from the south of Italy—Calabria and Sicily—are full bodied and dry, while those from the northeast, Veneto and the Alto Adige, are leaner with more acidity and bite than the southern wines.

The parish church of Marano di
Valpolicella in the Veneto wine region.

Whatever your taste in rosé, it is reassuring to know that wherever you find yourself in Italy, you won't be far from a glass of rosé.

PINK CHOICES

3

A word about the tasting notes. First of all, the wines are rated not just for one vintage but for performance over several vintages. That's why there are no vintage dates given in the notes. With a few exceptions, all the wineries here have proven quality over several vintages.

There is no intention here to make this a "complete" guide to rosé. That would require several volumes. What I have looked for are the highlights, the best from each region. Some regions have more entries than others because the wines are more readily available.

There are no number ratings here. There is no way anyone can pin a number between 0 and 100 on a wine and make it meaningful. Wine is a living, changing creature, not to be assigned a number and wait in line. The only ratings given here are from one to five stars. Right. The familiar Yelp system. It works. You will find few five stars here and even fewer one or two stars. However, every wine listed is worth trying or it would not be included in Pink Choices.

Warning! This is not a shopping list. You need not check off items and pop them in your cart. The Pink Choices here are offered simply as a rough guide, a pointer in the right direction. In the end, you must let your own taste be your guide.

Enjoy!

CHAMPAGNE AND SPARKLING WINE

ANTECH EMOTION

A bright and inviting Crémant de Limoux Brut from Languedoc. The wine shows crisp strawberry and cherry fruit, making it an excellent apéritif but also a good match with Asian cuisine, especially Thai. Or, you could forget the food and just party down with this lively bubbly.* * *

CAMPO VIEJO

This Brut non-vintage Cava from a top Rioja house offers luscious fruit up front with good bubble action right through the long finish. It is made from Trepat, an obscure Spanish grape grown mostly in Catalonia and often used in rosé blends (note that this is not a Rioja DO wine). An excellent apéritif and a good companion with young blue cheese or a bowl of spiced olives.* * *

CHARLES HEIDSIECK RESERVE ROSÉ

A balanced wine with sturdy tannins that help carry opening flavors of light red cherry and lychee through to a long finish. There is good acidity here and a fine interplay of minerality and fruit. The wine is full bodied, so it does go well with food, especially tapa-style plates like salami or a light fish paste such as taramosalata.* * *

DOMAINE CARNEROS

A stylish vintage-dated rosé sparkling wine, rare in California, that is a pleasure to hang out with. There are rounded aromas of red berries with a touch of lime on the opening. In the mouth the wine develops depth and complexity with a dash of plums and ripe berries. This wine will age for as much as a decade, so treat it with the respect it deserves. Goes well with roast duck, grilled salmon, or good friends around the table.* * * *

DOMAINE CHANDON

In 1973, Domaine Chandon was the first French-owned sparkling wine house established in California. The regular bottling of Chandon rosé is priced to please. It is also pleasing on the palate with intense ripe strawberry and red cherry fruit, building to a creamy and long finish. The top-of-the-line Étoile sparkler is an elegant wine, with supple plum and raspberry flavors, finishing with a rather mysterious and very satisfying hint of chocolate. The regular bottling is a good all around apéro/tapas wine, matching with a wide range of flavors. The Étoile pairs well with cheese, chocolate and your best friend.* * *–* * * *

DOPFF & IRION CRÉMANT D'ALSACE

This elegant dry brut rosé is a perfect apéritif, but it has the firmness to carry on throughout the meal. It is an especially good match with rice dishes, like risotto or paella. The opening aromas focus on red berry fruit with a touch of citrus. The finish is long, with lingering red fruit.* * *

DVX DOMAINE MUMM NAPA

This top-shelf sparkling wine was named to honor the founder of the winery. In 1976 Guy Devaux was sent from the mother house in France to find the right site to make bubbly in California. He nailed it. The first vintage under the Domaine Mumm was released in 1983 and they have been doing it right ever since. There is elegant fruit backed with a bright acidity that extends the long finish. Tasted with grilled salmon in a miso-mustard sauce. Excellent. Also makes a pleasing pleasure-driven apéro.* * * * *

GÉRARD BERTRAND

Crémant de Limoux Chardonnay, Chenin Blanc and Pinot Noir come together in this blend to produce a delightful sparkler, well-balanced and lively with a profusion of delicate bubbles and a long finish, with strawberry and raspberry fruit dominating. The vineyards, in the Limoux AOC in Languedoc, are some of the highest in southeastern France at between 800 and 1500 feet and are influenced by both Atlantic and Mediterranean breezes. Very good apéro but also excellent with grilled fish.* * * *

GUSTAVE LORENTZ CRÉMANT D'ALSACE

An elegant apéritif with bright minerality and a lively fruit base that encourages a second glass. It is an excellent match with raw oysters, spiced nuts, or a mild cheddar cheese.* *

HUBER HUGO

A pleasing everyday sparkling wine from Austria that performs well above its $13–$15 price point. It opens with delicate cranberry fruit with a spicy bite. There is a touch of strawberry and a light sprinkling of cloves in the mid-palate. It closes with a whiff of sweetness. An ideal apéro but with good acidity and grip could match well with chicken or grilled fish. It is a blend of Zweigelt, the most widely planted red grape in Austria, and Pinot Noir. The wine is made by 10th-generation winegrower Markus Huber and is part of the Hugo line of wines especially designed to be on the table every day.* *

JEIO DESIDERIO

This spumante brut from the Veneto delivers the pure pleasure we often expect in an Italian bubbly but rarely get. It's a real party animal. A pale pink in the glass, the aroma ranges from light citrus to ripe peach. The flavors linger through a long and dry finish. This is an ideal apéritif but will also play well with tapas, smoked meats, and blue cheese.* * *

KORBEL BRUT ROSÉ

A luscious bubbly from a reliable and affordable Sonoma producer. Sip it as a delicious apéro with just the right smack of sugar at the finish to keep you smiling. One of Korbel's better efforts.* * *

KRUG BRUT ROSÉ

Undoubtedly the Queen of Champagnes—and at a royal price, of course—it opens with a silky mouth feel, fresh and delicate. The fruit is somewhat restrained by a brisk acidity that refreshes the palate while you pour a second glass. It would match with a variety of foods, but why? It is so good standing alone that it's best to simply sip and enjoy.* * * * *

LOUIS BOUILLOT CRÉMANT DE BOURGOGNE, PERLE D'AURORE BRUT

Enjoying a glass of this rosé is like welcoming an old friend, someone fun to hang out with, open and refreshing in conversation. It's a blend of Pinot Noir and Gamay. On the palate, the fruit shines, polished with a brisk acidity with just a touch of sweetness at the end coupled with an intriguing earthiness from the Pinot Noir. Try a solo glass or with grilled fish, chicken, or perhaps even a lamb chop.* * *

LOUIS ROEDERER CRISTAL

Easily one of the top rosé sparklers, this champagne offers complex flavors—intense and full-bodied. The lingering finish is an elegant homage to Pinot Noir. The vintage version can take a bit of age.* * * *

MONT MARCAL

I have to admit up front that I am a fool for cava and will often choose it over champagne, but this brut cava needs no apologies. It is made from the Trepat grape, a rare red-skinned grape probably native to Catalonia. It offers distinctive flavors with bright acidity and lingering fruit at a quality point equal to most non-vintage champagnes. Splendid as an apéritif or served with nuts, olives, and cheese. It also matches well with spicy pan-Asian dishes.* * *

PALMER & CO RESERVE NV

A bright and inviting rosé champagne that is a treat for the palate. It opens with a rich and creamy mousse balanced by yummy strawberry fruit, followed by a spicy center. The finish is long and satisfying. This is a non-vintage champagne, but it will age nicely for several years, gaining more richness on the finish. On the other hand, it's hard to resist opening this delicious bubbly as soon as you feel the need for a glass of champagne.* * *

RAVENTOS BLANC DE NIT

This delightful Spanish sparkler comes with good cred. Grapes were first planted on the Raventos estate in Catalonia in 1496, so the family has had plenty of time to get it right. This is an elegant and complex cava, with soft red berry fruit, good acidity, and minerality. Try this with sliced ham or other tapas, or enjoy a glass as an apéritif.* * * *

ROEDERER ESTATE

The L'Ermitage Tête de Cuvée Rosé is made only from exceptional vintages from the first pressing of the grapes, which are all from Roederer's vineyards in the Anderson Valley of Mendocino County, a few miles from the Pacific. It is an outstanding wine, easily among the best California sparklers. It is a pale salmon color with a creamy mouth feel and a supple finish that keeps delivering through a long aftertaste. Roederer also makes a very good non-vintage brut bubbly which is splendid and just right for your daily table. Both wines pair well with grilled halibut or salmon, and are, of course, just fine all alone.* * * *

SCHRAMSBERG

Schramsberg is at the head of the class for California sparkling wine. The Napa winery makes four sparkling rosés, with the vintage J. Schram leading the way. It's an elegant wine with long lasting flavors and a creamy richness. Match with fresh crab, roasted pork, grilled fish, or enjoy on its own as a fabulous apéritif. The Schramsberg Vintage brut is a complex wine, featuring bright Pinot Noir fruit with good depth and deep flavors. The Mirabelle non-vintage rosé is bursting with ripe fruit and makes an ideal apéritif. Schramsberg also makes Qurencia, a house specialty dedicated to the memory of winery founder Jack Davies. Sales of Qurencia—a Spanish term that can be roughly translated "love of one's home"—benefit Napa land preservation.* * *–* * * * *

VEUVE CLICQUOT

Go for the elegant vintage brut rosé and you will treat yourself to one of the world's top sparkling wines. Crisp fruit on the palate, followed by a long finish. This champagne has become the gold standard for many and it deserves to be. A bonus is that it will age and develop in the bottle- if you can have the patience to hold on for a few years. Good luck with that.* * * * *

CALIFORNIA AND OREGON

AUBICHON CELLARS

Winemaker Jim Sanders made his mark with outstanding Pinot Noir from Le Cadeau Vineyards in Oregon's Willamette Valley. Sanders, who takes pride in what he calls "time inefficient winemaking," clearly knows how to deal with the pink stuff as well. His rosé of Pinot Gris is superb. There is abundant fruit with an emphasis on plum and strawberries with a creamy, rich mouth feel. The long finish takes a toasty turn with a touch of vanilla. This wine has the structure to take on pork chops and leg of lamb.* * *

BECKMEN PMV

A lively and pleasing rosé made from Grenache grown in the Santa Ynez Valley appellation of Santa Barbara County. It opens with strawberry and guava fruits with a creamy edge. As the wine develops on the palate there are hints of watermelon and pomegranate backed by a balancing acidity. This is a good wine to match with a wide range of food, but especially roast chicken or grilled lamb.* * *

BENESSERE VINEYARDS

This deeply flavored Rosato di Sangiovese from Napa is extraordinarily full bodied, with a deep salmon color. Eyes closed, it could pass for a light red. Cherry and raspberries dominate the flavors, with a peppery spice on the finish. The wine would pair well with pasta (extra garlic, please), grilled fish (especially salmon), and shellfish.* * *

BENTON LANE

Made from estate-grown Pinot Noir in the Willamette Valley, this is serious and very good wine. The color is a fairly dark shade of pink with rich cranberry and cherry fruit layered with a touch of not-quite-ripe apple rounding out the intense opening flavors. The wine is supple, with a bright and fairly long follow-through. This wine will match with rich sauces, roast chicken, and grilled lamb. And it might even age a year or three.* * * * *

ROBERT BIALE VINEYARDS ROSATO

This bend of Sangiovese and Zinfandel hits all of the right palate points. There's a generous serving of spicy fruit, including strawberries. The finish is long with wraparound flavors, including another spoonful or two of fresh strawberries. Altogether a real treat from an always reliable Napa winery. The Sangiovese, a grape of Italian origin, is from vines grown in warmer vineyards east of San Francisco Bay.* * * *

BLACKBIRD VINEYARDS ARRIVISTE

Winemaker Aaron Pott has taken time off from his own Pott Wines project, where his wines are on allocation, to make an impressive rosé for Blackbird in Napa. The wine is a blend of Cabernet Franc, Cabernet Sauvignon, and Merlot, made by the saignée method. Pott, who worked in France for several years, is clearly aiming for more upfront fruit—strawberries on the nose and opening followed by tart citrus with a side of cherry—than is common in French rosé, however. The wine has a stiffer backbone than is usual in California rosé, probably due to the saignée production. It may not be everyone's glass of rosé, but it takes itself seriously and is worth a look.* * *

BOKISCH

This Lodi winery specializes in wines made from Spanish grape varieties. The rosado of Garnacha is like a holiday in Spain. There's bright acidity against a backdrop of strawberry, raspberry, and a pleasing dash of watermelon. The finish is long with a touch of citrus. A lovely apéritif that can keep you company right through the meal. Particularly good with pork, especially slices of Spanish ham or grilled pork chops. Olé.* * * *

Bonny Doon Vin Gris de Cigare

It doesn't seem possible but this wine from Randall Grahm keeps getting better with every vintage. It is a blend of Rhône varieties, dominated by Grenache Noir and Grenache Gris. It is rich on the palate without being overwhelming, with intense strawberry fruit shaped by a pleasing minerality with a minty background. This wine has the strength to match with pork, lamb, almost anything from the grill, although Randall likes his with raw oysters.* * * * *

Bouchaine

This Vin Gris of Pinot Noir is a show stopper. It will make your palate sit up and take notice. Made from estate Pinot Noir in the Carneros region of California, it has rich, intense fruit and great length. There is nothing wimpy about this wine. It has a smoky edge that will match with barbecue, a spicy Asian dish, or whatever you want to put beside it.* * * * *

Broc Cellars Love Rosé

The name of the wine says it all, right? It is a gorgeous wine, both in the glass and on the palate. The grapes— Valdiguié, Grenache Gris, and Zinfandel—are all from dry-farmed organic vines. The opening peach flavors continue through a long finish. Love Rosé is a good wine to party with or linger over with an aged goat cheese. Broc, one of Napa's urban wineries, has a winner here.****

BRYTER ESTATES JUBILEE

They call the wine Jubilee in celebration of pink wine. Made from Pinot Noir grown in the cool Sonoma Coast AVA, it's a very pale shade of pink, almost in the peach zone. Elegant and balanced, with lingering citrus and raspberry fruit, the wine offers a crisp acidity and a creamy finish. Try with an aged blue cheese.***

CACHE CREEK VINEYARDS

A rosé of Cabernet Sauvignon from Lake County that shows good varietal fruit with a splash of watermelon and bing cherry. It is a "pretty" wine, both for the eye and the palate, with a medium finish and balanced fruit. This shows best as an apéritif or with a cheddar-style cheese.**

CAKEBREAD VIN DE PORCHE ANDERSON VALLEY

Mostly Pinot Noir with a dash of Syrah from Napa vineyards. This is a classic style rosé. Fruit forward on the nose and palate with cherry and raspberry tones, good acidity, fresh and lively right through the finish. It's wine for an apéro on the front porch (get it?) but will also pair well with a wide range of food. We sampled it with a Korean grilled chicken breast, heavy with chilies, and the wine paired brilliantly. It would also work well with grilled fish, summer salads and Mexican dishes. Bruce Cakebread suggests a dish of Manila clams with Andouille sausage.****

CLIF FAMILY WINERY ROSÉ OF GRENACHE

An engaging Grenache rosé. The color is light salmon with full upfront fruit featuring a touch of lime and pear, backed by a bold acidity, leading to a lingering finish. Clif, a Napa destination winery complete with a food truck, has just recently been converted to the Pink cause. They are off to a good start.***

CORAZÓN

Cathy Corison should be declared a national treasure. She makes one of California's best Cabernets at her Napa winery, so it hardly seems fair that she also makes such good rosé. This rosé is made by the saignée method—bleeding off red juice from the Cabernet Sauvignon. Those who frown on saignée rosé are way off base with this one. There are complex layers of flavor fairly leaping from the glass—bright red cherry with brisk acidity—leading to a long finish. Great with grilled meats, roast chicken, or enjoyed on its own.* * * * *

CORNERSTONE CELLARS CORALLINA

Absolutely top-drawer rosé of Syrah from the Oak Knoll AVA of Napa. A vivid pink in the glass, the wine opens with ripe raspberry and strawberry fruit, balanced by a brisk acidity, seasoned with a dash of white pepper and a pinch of sage. The finish is full bodied and satisfying with the opening fruit lingering and rich. Try with grilled lamb or chicken. It snuggles up nicely to fish tacos as well.* * * *

DASHE

A pleasing blend of Grenache and Zinfandel from vineyards in the Dry Creek Valley of Sonoma County from an always reliable producer. There's bright strawberry and raspberry fruit with good acidity, leading to a long and layered finish supported by a lean minerality. A great match with shellfish, raw oysters, or any sort of seafood stew.* * *

DEL RIO

From the Rouge River Valley in southern Oregon, a rosé of Grenache Syrah shows a light red color in the glass. The wine has long and vibrant fruit with strawberry and melon dominating. The finish offers layered flavors, fairly long with herbal tones. The wine has the structure to pair with grilled chicken or fish and is especially good with a cheddar-style cheese.* * *

Del Rio also makes a semi-sweet bubbly based on Muscat and Riesling with a touch of Cabernet Franc. It is a lively apéro.* *

DONKEY & GOAT ISABEL'S CUVÉE

This wine, made from old vine Mendocino County Grenache, will make you sit up and take notice. There are layers of flavor with ripe berry fruit held in check by bright minerality leading to an edgy and long finish. The urban winery (Berkeley) has been making this wine for several years and it simply keeps getting better and better. It would pair well with grilled lamb or chicken and is the perfect match for salmon.* * * *

EDMUNDS ST. JOHN BONE-JOLLY GAMAY NOIR ROSÉ

From his winery in Berkeley, Steve Edmunds has roamed California for decades looking for vineyards that deliver wine from a place, terroir based wines, not market based. This luscious and fresh rosé is from a vineyard in the Sierra Foothills, planted especially for him. The fruit, intense and lingering, hits all the right points, inviting another glass. Good as an apéro or with a wide selection of food, especially grilled salmon. A pure *vin du plaisir*.* * * *

FIDDLEHEAD CELLARS

Kathy Joseph crafts an outstanding rosé from Pinot Noir grown in the Santa Rita Hills AVA in Santa Barbara County. It opens on a spicy note and moves on to fresh strawberry with good acidity on the finish. A fun wine to hang out with but serious enough for a long term relationship.* * * *

FIRESTONE VINEYARD

A Grenache-based rosé from Santa Ynez Valley in the Central Coast AVA shows bright red berry colors in the glass and a friendly burst of raspberry and melon in the mouth. This is a pink to enjoy on its on or with fresh fruit, cheese, cured olives, and maybe a little chicken paté. Finishes with a pinch of sugar. Yummy.* *

FORTUNATI ROSÉ OF SYRAH

Made from estate grown Napa Syrah, this light salmon pink wine has a forward palate of strawberries and cherries backed by a pleasing minerality. There is a forest floor, dried leaf edge to the aroma, to be expected in a Syrah. Put a couple of bottles of this in the 'fridge and fire up the grill.* * *

HANNA

A refreshing blend of Malbec and Pinot Noir from Sonoma County that offers intense melon and strawberry aromas on the opening with a nectarine and raspberry finish with just a hint of sweetness. The closing flavors echo the opening fruit and linger vividly. A good apéro, this also matches nicely with cured pork, chicken, and Mexican cuisine.* * *

HEITZ CELLAR GRIGNOLINO ROSÉ

This Napa Valley classic shows abundant fruit with a touch of citrus. There is an engaging acidity that embraces the uplifted fruit and sets it doing cartwheels across the palate. Perfectly balanced and eager to please. The wine is in limited production, so if you find it, grab a half-dozen bottles and you will be truly in the pink.* * * *

HUSCH VIN GRIS OF PINOT NOIR

The Husch family were vinous pioneers in Anderson Valley, a cool-growing region in Mendocino County on the North Coast of California. The first crush was in 1971. In 1979, the winery and vineyards were bought by the Oswald family, who had been making wine in the Santa Clara Valley, south of San Francisco. They got off to a good start and have maintained a high standard. This is a gorgeous wine, appealing to the eye with a deep strawberry color. The opening fruit tones pick up the strawberry theme with a touch of ripe cherry and run with it to a long and satisfying finish.***

INMAN FAMILY ENDLESS CRUSH

A delightful Pinot Noir rosé from the Russian River Valley of Sonoma County. The color is deep strawberry, almost a light red wine. The nose and opening flavors show a herbal complexity of sage, rosemary and tarragon. The center is dark plum and ripe strawberry. This rosé, from a Pinot Noir specialist, invites a second glass. Maybe a third.***

JANA

This supple and bright rosé of Pinot Noir is winemaker Scott Harvey's tribute to his wife, Jana (Harvey also makes Tickle Me Pink). Made from Napa grapes, this is an elegant wine with crisp minerality supporting raspberry and pomegranate fruit. The finish goes on and on, echoing the opening flavors. Match this rosé with raw oysters, grilled lamb, and a creamy blue cheese.* * * *

J.K. CARRIERE

Despite the unlikely name of Glass White Pinot Noir, this is an outstanding wine from the Willamette Valley of Oregon, crafted by Oregon maverick Jim Prosser. Prosser is part of the new wave of rosé producers who are changing the image of the wine in Oregon. It is reminiscent of the great rosés from Alsace, with vibrant acidity to balance the red berry and citrus fruit. The long finish is spiced by a dash of white pepper and lychee. Enjoy on its own or pair this with a table of mezze or tapas.* * * *

J LOHR GESTURE

J Lohr is a much underrated California treasure. Because Lohr makes a lot of wine and sells it at a reasonable price, many dismiss it as an "everyday" wine. And just what is wrong with an everyday wine? The Gesture series is Lohr's homage to Rhône varietals and this rosé is a Grenache Noir and Grenache Blanc blend. It opens with intense strawberry and pear aromas that follow through on the palate. There is excellent acidity and a refreshing tartness on the finish. A great match with shellfish or any grilled meat, especially if it has a Mexican flavor.****

KALE

A superb rosé from a relative newcomer. Kale Anderson and his wife Ranko began making small lots of wine from a few Northern California vineyards in 2008. The rosé, made from Grenache with a splash of Mourvédre, is from a hillside vineyard in Sonoma. It is a brilliant wine showing strawberry and watermelon notes with an underlying minerality that brings it together. Keep an eye on Kale. There is five-star potential here.****

KEELER

A superb Pinot Noir rosé from biodynamic and organic estate vineyards in Oregon. The wine is a bright salmon color opening to vivid raspberry fruit with a sprinkling of light spice—cinnamon and a hint of nutmeg. The finish is long and rounded with good acidity. Match this with a risotto. Splendid.****

LANGE

A terroir-focused estate in the Dundee Hills AVA of Oregon. In a typical year, the Lange family bottles up to ten different Pinot Noirs, searching out special vineyard sites to showcase the variety. Their rosé, as site specific as the red wine, is a deep ruby color in the glass with vivid fruit and a spicy finish. Pair this with Asian or Mexican cuisine, or with ripe blue cheese.* * *

LIQUID FARMS HAPPY CANYON

One of California's best from the Vogelzang Vineyard in the Santa Rita Hills AVA of Santa Barbara County. Mourvédre with a dash of Grenache. The opening eases in with hints of basil leading into a center of orange zest, a hint of pepper and red fruit, and finishes on the opening herbal note with spikes of minerality. With all that action going on, it still finishes balanced and elegant. A very Euro-centric rosé, and more power to it. Just give it a light chill and serve with grilled chicken or quail, a salmon fillet, or even pork.* * * * *

LONG MEADOW RANCH

A top Napa Cabernet house has turned to rosé with good results. Their first effort is a rosé of Pinot Noir from Anderson Valley in Mendocino County. It has good opening flavors of tropical fruit and lime with a solid structure, much like a red wine. The finish is long and layered. It's delightful on its own but would match well with roast duck or grilled lamb, followed by a chocolate truffle. It earns three stars for openers but keep an eye on Long Meadow rosé. It will probably get even better.* * *

LEFT COAST CELLARS

A lively and delicious rosé of Pinot Noir from the Willamette Valley in Oregon, ground zero for so many outstanding Pinot Noir wines. It's an attractive wine, both in the glass—light salmon color—and on the palate, with bright citrus and melon fruit balanced by a brisk acidity. The finish is fairly long with a satisfying wrap of flavors. Serve this with pasta in a light cream sauce, grilled fish, or a young goat cheese.* * *

LUCAS & LEWELLEN TOCCATA RAMATO

A lively Pinot Grigio from cool-climate vines in Santa Barbara County, a few miles from the Pacific. With fresh berry and melon fruit, it is reminiscent of the toccata (copper colored) wines of northeast Italy and the Veneto. A touch of minerality keeps the fruit in pleasing balance with the acidity, and the wine works as an apéro or with dried meats, cured olives, and cheese.* * *

NAVARRO VINEYARDS

An excellent rosé of Pinot Noir is a recent addition to Navarro's portfolio of wine. Navarro has made outstanding Pinot Noir in the Anderson Valley of Mendocino County for decades, so it is no surprise that when they turned their attention to rosé it would be very good as well. The wine has strawberry and ripe raspberry fruit, balanced by a zesty acidity. It would pair well with sliced ham and other cured pork as well as fish and chicken.* * * *

PEDRONCELLI

The Pedroncelli family still operates the winery founded in Sonoma during The Prohibition, when they sold grapes to home winemakers. Wink, wink. Zinfandel has always been the go-to wine for Pedroncelli, and this is a brilliant rosé based on Zinfandel. It has a crispy spice with a touch of pepper and citrus. There is good acidity combined with generous fruit on the finish. This wine will pair with almost any spicy dish and is especially good with an Indian curry * * *

PINE RIDGE ENCANTADO

This Napa winery is known for its outstanding Cabernet Sauvignon, so this pink blend of Merlot and Cabernet Sauvignon gives them a chance to have a little fun, right? It is a brilliant watermelon color in the glass with opening aromas of watermelon and strawberry. Nectarine and citrus follow the watermelon on the palate to a lively finish. An ideal apéro but also match with shellfish, especially raw oysters.* * *

CHÂTEAU POTELLE, VGS

This is a fun wine to hang out with, a true elbow bender, and what more could you ask for? Plus, it passed my peanut butter test. Enjoyed it first with a bowl of olives, a safe food choice for a pink wine, followed that with Down Home Lunch #3: a peanut butter, pickle relish, and mayo sandwich. It's true. On the more wine geek side, the wine, made from Cinsault, offers broad wraparound flavors of spicy fruit followed by a long finish. Make that crunchy peanut butter. And a second glass of VGS.* *

PRESQU'ILE

A bright and lively rosé of Pinot Noir from the Santa Maria Valley on the Central Coast. There is intense strawberry fruit with good acidity to carry the fruit through a long finish. A perfect apéritif but also works well with seafood, especially clams or grilled Monterey squid.**

RAINSTORM

A bright and cheerful rosé called Silver Linings—Rainstorm, Silver Linings, get it?—produced by Banfi, the international wine giant that brought you Riunite, designed to spotlight Oregon Pinot Noir. This bottling of Pinot Noir rosé from Oregon's Willamette and Umpqua AVAs opens with vivid strawberry fruit, leading to a lively finish with good acidity to match with a variety of foods. Try it with a spicy pasta.**

Y. ROUSSEAU

You don't see a lot of rosé made from Tannat. If this wine is any example, there should be a lot more of it. Yannick Rousseau, the winemaker and owner, has the cred, coming from Gascony in southwest France where Tannat is an important wine grape. In the glass, the color is a lovely pale salmon. The nose is all about strawberries and watermelon with a touch of lime zest. On the palate, the opening aromas are picked up with an added herbal note and a more pronounced lime/ citrus flavor and a pinch of white pepper. Rousseau is one of the new wave of Napa urban wineries—think warehouse and loading docks and no chateau, thank you—and the Tannat is grown especially for rosé from vineyards in Solano County, just east of San Francisco Bay. The wine has good structure and would match with a wide range of foods including grilled lamb, which may be the first choice.* * * * *

SAFFRON FIELDS

A splendid Pinot Noir based rosé from Oregon's Willamette Valley. The color is the deep pink of strawberries, which pop up again in the opening aromas and in the mouth. There's also a rich mélange of plum and tart cherry with enough acidity to keep this an honest food wine. Try with a paella, risotto, or a creamy dessert. It's also a winner on its own.* * * *

ST. SUPÉRY

A balanced and bright rosé made from the five Bordeaux red varieties from Napa estate vineyards. There is vivid strawberry and raspberry fruit with an earthy base of dry rose petals. The finish is long and intense. A perfect rosé for grilled salmon.* * *

SOKOL BLOSSER

An elegant Pinot Noir rosé made from organically farmed grapes. Sokol Blosser has been making outstanding wines in Oregon since 1971, and this wine is no exception. A pale copper color, the wine has refreshing Pinot Noir fruit with good acidity to carry the lively flavors. The wine makes an attractive and palate-pleasing apéritif but also pairs well with pan-seared fish or creamy pastas.* * *

ELIZABETH SPENCER

The husband-wife team of Elizabeth Pressler and Spencer Graham make two very good rosés, among other outstanding wines. The Mendocino Rosé is made from old vine Grenache in Mendocino County. The opening aromas are astonishing—ripe apricot and fresh strawberry. In the mouth, the strawberry theme continues, with a touch of citrus and white peach. The finish is zesty and extended. A rosé of Pinot Noir comes from a cool climate vineyard a few miles north of San Francisco Bay. Look for strawberry and raspberry aromas in the opening with grapefruit and lime kept in check, with lively acidity on the palate. Both wines have the structure to pair with red meats as well as such standard rosé fair as grilled fish and soft blue cheese. Overall rating of * * * *.

STOLLER

Another outstanding wine from the Dundee Hills AVA in the Willamette Valley in Oregon. Bill Stoller grew up on the Stoller family farm long before any vines were planted there. In the 1940s, it was a turkey farm. It wasn't until the 1990s that he took control of the family estate and began planting vines. It was a good idea. There are plenty of turkeys in the world, not nearly enough good wines. The Stoller rosé of Pinot Noir is an elegant wine, brimming with lush red grapefruit and a touch of melon and ripe strawberries. The finish is long and mouth filling. The wine, fine on its own, matches well with a light cheese pasta, grilled salmon, or a cheddar style cheese.* * *

TICKLE ME PINK

This is an all-day, all-night wine. From a late breakfast to a post-midnight glass. Made by Scott Harvey of Jana wines, it opens with fruit tones of crisp pear and an edge of citrus and stays fresh and lively from the opening sip through a long just off-dry finish. Color this wine yummy and pair it with good friends.* * *

TWILL CELLARS MOLLY'S VINEYARD

This rich and deeply flavored rosé of organically grown and dry farmed Pinot Noir is an elegant and vivid wine from the Willamette Valley in Oregon. The color is pale copper with aromas of citrus and cherry. With long-lasting flavors carried by intense minerality, this wine has the structure to match with big flavors. Don't be afraid to pair with grilled lamb or pork, or aged Gouda.* * * *

A ROSÉ FAN

Just to step outside the statistics box, we went looking for that well-known man (or woman) on the street who is a rosé drinker.

We found Katie Blum, a thirty-something Oklahoma-born New Yorker. Blum, a journalist who works for Dateline NBC, said she has a "very social lifestyle, as most New Yorkers do." She likes to go to sports events and Broadway shows and says she also enjoys "drinking wine with my girlfriends, especially rosé."

"I started drinking rosé after a trip to Napa," Blum said. She was first attracted to rosé because "I found it the right wine for rooftop drinks on a hot day in New York. But now I might open a bottle of rosé any time of the year."

Blum said all of her friends drink rosé. "We had a rosé-only party this summer at my apartment. Everyone had to bring a bottle of rosé and an appetizer."

As for pricing, since Blum lives in Manhattan she probably spends a bit above the average on her rosé. "Usually about $12 a glass. That's about the normal price. For a bottle, anywhere from $25 to $50 in a restaurant and around $20 to $35 in a retail shop."

Her favorite pinks? "I really love the Vin de Porche from Cakebread in Napa. It is very flavorful yet crisp. I also enjoy Whispering Angel and Miraval," Blum said.

Good choices, Ms. Blum. Carry on, pink.

UNION WINE COMPANY

An elbow bender, show-me-the-way-to-the-beach kind of wine, but no harm done and plenty of pleasure. Union's Underwood label is all about having fun with wine. This rosé is an unusual blend of Pinot Gris, Riesling, Muscat, Pinot Noir and Syrah from several different Oregon vineyards. It's all about watermelon, strawberry, and peach fruit and is sure to put a smile to your face. It is also available in a 375ml can, same wine as the bottle. Why? Because they can.*

WIND GAP

This Sonoma County winery based in Sebastopol, which used to be called the apple capital before winemakers moved in, specializes in single vineyard wines, usually from cool climates. The Pinot Gris could easily be mistaken for an "orange" wine from the bright color in the glass. Long maceration on the skins has led to spicy, rather exotic, fruit with flavors of white peach and lychee balanced by lively tannins. A lovely apéritif, but also plays nicely with roast duck or chicken and spicy Asian or Mexican dishes.* * *

YAMHILL VALLEY VINEYARDS

A happy blend of Pinot Noir and Pinot Blanc from the Willamette Valley AVA. We are in apéritif country with this refreshing and delicious wine. However, it pairs with more than swimming pools and beaches. Try it with a creamy pasta dish or a chilled gazpacho.* *

WINE BY JOE

A delightful rosé of Pinot Noir from the Dobbes Family Estate winery in the Willamette Valley. Winemaker Joe Dobbes bottles several value-for-money wines, such as this one, to put a good daily wine on the table. There is vibrant peach and strawberry fruit leading to a medium finish with balanced and full mouth feel. The wine pairs well with grilled chicken, salmon, and lightly spiced Asian dishes.* * *

YORKVILLE CELLARS VIN D'UNE NUIT

The name translates, according to the winery, as "one night stand," which could also be read as a "quickie." Perhaps closer to the original French is "wine of one night," which refers to one night of skin contact before the grapes are pressed. And that is grape skin they are talking about. At any rate, despite the rather loose translation, the wine is marvelous. It has everything you could ask—strawberry, melon, citrus, excellent acidity, and a long finish. This is a serious rosé that just wants to have fun. And, as a bonus, the grapes, from the Yorkville Highlands AVA, are organically farmed and the price is under $20. Buy it by the case.****

FRANCE

Provençe

MAISON SAINT AIX

A taste of summer, beginning with the pale pink vision in the glass followed by the vibrant opening and mid-palate flavors of ripe orange with a hint of fig and cherries with maybe a dash of thyme. Lovely wine right through to the long engaging finish with an intriguing smoky flavor at the end, reminiscent of mezcal. Yes, really. Excellent with roast chicken or grilled rabbit. Have a few glasses on the terrace before lunch. Terrific wine.*****

DOMAINE SAINT ANDRIEU CÔTES DE PROVENCE

An understated rosé opening with pale red berry tones, followed by a hint of strawberry and citrus notes—lime and lemon—with a dash of cloves. The finish is pleasing, with the strawberry popping up again to add depth. The winery was purchased in 2003 by Jean-Paul and Nancy Bignon, owners of Château Talbot, a cru classé winery in the Médoc. They wanted to make a rosé, so Provence was the clear choice.* * *

CHÂTEAU BARBANAU L'INSTANT

This rosé from Côtes de Provençe organic grapes offers about all anyone could ask for in a Provençal rosé. The color is pale peach. It opens with lively fruit and bright minerality. The mid-palate flavors and finish are uplifted and intense with layers of red berry and citrus fruit and framing acidity. Excellent apéro but also good with Mexican, spicy Asian, or try it with a south Indian curry. Oh, my!* * * *

Barbanau also offers Girafe Vert (Green Giraffe), a second wine from organic grapes with the slogan Go Green. It's a true *vin du plaisir*, sure to make you right with the world.* * *

CHÂTEAU HENRI BONNAUD TERRE PROMISE

There is a lot to like in this lively wine, a 50-50 blend of Grenache and Syrah. The opening fruit tones and spice notes are inviting and the mouthfeel is full and easy to like. An apéro-friendly wine for everyday drinking. Potential for three stars here or even more.**

Maison Belle Claire

A very inviting opening, focusing on ripe strawberry fruit with good acidity, creating a bright and balanced, if somewhat simple wine, and there's nothing wrong with that. You can enjoy it as a very satisfying apéro without going all geeky.*

Château de Brigue

No way to go wrong here. A very good daily pink. The wine is deeply colored with bright fresh strawberry and cherry fruit, very refreshing. A blend of Grenache, Cinsault and Mourvédre, the wine finishes long and balanced. Good news is that it is in the $10 range. Get in a good supply, not just for the summer but for all seasons.***

Le Caprice de Clementine

This wine brings a smile to the face and joy to the palate. It's the wine that everyone imagines when thinking of Provençal rosé. A blend of Grenache and Cinsault, it opens with welcoming fruit—red cherry and citrus—and an intensity of flavor seldom tasted in a pink wine. The close is long and echoes the opening fruit. The winery is only a few miles from St. Tropez and all that lovely Mediterranean sunshine. It will be waiting for you in the glass.* * * * *

CHÂTEAU FERRY LACOMBE MIRA

The Ferry family established this Provençal winery in 1442, near the city of Aix-en-Provence. Rosé is a house specialty and Mira, a blend of Grenache, Cinsault and Vermentino, is a good example of why the estate is so highly regarded. It is an elegant wine, light pink in the glass with a delicate nose and citrus aromas on the opening. The fruit is laid on with a light hand, spiced by a brisk minerality. Splendid apéro wine but also a match with grilled fish and roast chicken.* * * *

DOMAINE DE LA FOUQUETTE ROSÉ D'AURORE

This wine, from the heart of the Côtes de Provençe AOC, is a wine that demands a second glass. It's the usual Provençal blend, Grenache and Cinsault with a dash of Vermentino, called Rolle in France, with tangy broad cherry and red berry fruit punctuated by a spike of minerality. It's the kind of wine that keeps coming back in the palate memory the day after you try it. More, please. Aurore, by the way, is the name of the daughter of owners Isabelle and Jean-Pierre Daziano.* * * *

HAEDUS

An attractive wine in the glass with pale pink shading into peach. The wine, from Château Ferry Lacombe, opens with intense red fruit flavors mingled with pear, peach, and a dash of white pepper, The mouthfeel is full, balanced by good acidity and minerality. The finish is long with opening fruit flavors looping back. The name means young goat and is connected with ancient Mediterranean myths. This wine, however, is for real. Pair with grilled fish, white meat, or best of all, paella.* * * * *

MONCIGALE

Century-old winery now owned by drinks giant Marie Bizzard produces reliable and sometimes outstanding rosé. The Aix-en-Provence line is especially good, with an excellent balance and flavor profile of floral and fruit aromas; ripe strawberries and raspberries dominate. The wine has a layered finish, with bright echoes of the opening fruit.* * * *

CHÂTEAU REAL D'OR

The winery was established following the war in 1946. In 2010, new owners updated the vineyards and the winery, and the new wines are showing very well indeed. Best is the Monte Carlo *cépage*, a bright and cheerful blend of Grenache and Syrah. The wine opens with pleasing fruit backed by brisk acidity that keeps the flavors uplifted and full. The finish is long with a rich mouthfeel, thanks to the generous splash of Syrah.* * *

CHÂTEAU DU ROUET ESTÉRELLE

This rosé from a showcase estate offers lively fruit, a tasty mélange of red and dark berries with an emphasis on cherries and strawberries. The high percentage of the Tibourenc grape gives the wine a wraparound aroma of garrigue. The Tibourenc grape is of obscure origin, possibly Greece or somewhere in the Middle East. It gives rosé an added dimension but is seldom planted because of susceptibility to disease and resultant crop loss. Hats off to Rouet for taking a chance. The wine is an elegant beauty that hits all the palate pleasure points.* * *

DOMAINE SACHA LICHINE

Outstanding wines from a rock star winemaker. Under the Château d'Esclans label, there is Rock Angel and Whispering Angel. Rock Angel is a rounded and creamy wine with a spicy edge. Whispering Angel is more angular and understated but with a fine thread of flavor. Moving upscale is Garrus, a bolder shade of pink with good minerality hinting at wet stones or food cooked in a clay pot. The finish is long and rounded. Les Clans is a big wine with rich, full-bodied fruit tamed by a firm minerality. The "Angel" wines are very good apéritifs and as a match with lighter fish dishes. The Garrus and Les Clans are excellent with grilled meats or roast chicken.* * * *–* * * * *

DOMAINE SAINTE-LUCIE MiP

The initials signal Made in Provence and this is, indeed, a Provençal classic rosé. The typical Provençal rosé fruit is on hand, with an added touch of pear and floral notes. The wine is delicate, yet it would also be a good picnic companion, maybe with some mild cheddar and a book of lyric poetry. Open it up and give it a try. You won't regret it.* * *

L'Esprit de Sainte-Marguerite

Located in the village of La Londe-les-Maures, the scenic winery near the Mediterranean owns just under 200 acres (75 hectares) of organically farmed grapes on a clay and shale soil. The varieties are Cinsault, Grenache and Syrah, the classic triad for Provençal pink wines. It opens with delightful peach and pear wraparound flavors with a touch of raspberry for taste emphasis. It is a balanced and satisfying wine but a bit too low in acidity for four-star status.* * *

Château Saint-Maur Clos de Capelune

A subtle wine with opening aromas of white peach with a sprinkling of white pepper. As the wine opens, tones of citrus and apricot come into play with a balancing minerality. The wine has a firm structure, which means it is one of the rare rosés that could develop further with a year or three of aging. On the other hand, it is delicious as a young wine, so why wait? * * *

Unparalleled

A charming blend of Grenache, Syrah, and Vermentino from Coteaux d'Aix-en-Provence, the wine is a very light shade of pink in the glass with a touch of citrus on the nose. It finishes fairly long with a spicy citrus note. It goes well with grilled fish or chicken and would be just the wine for a round of tapas, beginning with olives and ending with a fresh goat or sheep cheese.* * *

Languedoc-Roussillon

DOMAINE DE BILA HAUT

Another outstanding quality-for-value pink from Roussillon. This wine, with focused and uplifted fruit and bright minerality, is a Chapoutier project. Chapoutier, a Rhône producer and négociant, has been expanding into Roussillon (as well as Australia and Portugal) in a search for quality wines, based on biodynamic farming. The wine's firm structure and broad flavors make it a particularly good match with winter stews, maybe a warming cassoulet, or grilled meats.* * *

CHÂTEAU COUPE ROSES

The winery makes two outstanding rosés from high elevation organic vineyards in the Minervois region of northern Languedoc. The Bastide bottling has great intensity of flavor with good acidity leading to a long finish. The Granaxa bottling (Granaxa is Grenache in the old Occitan language) is finished in barrel, rare for a Languedoc rosé, and is capable of aging for two to three years. It is a rich wine with a silky texture leading to a long and layered finish.* * *—* * * *

Domaine de Fontsainte Gris de Gris

A rosé from the Corbieres mountains of Roussillon, a few miles from the Mediterranean. It's a blend of several typical southeastern French varieties, with Grenache Gris taking the lead. The region was first planted to grapes by the Romans and the occasional Roman artifact turns up in the vineyard. More importantly, a lot of pleasure comes from the vineyard. There is intense red berry fruit and a lean minerality that keeps the palate refreshed. Another glass, please.* * * *

Château St. Jacques d'Albas

A seriously delicious rosé from an organic vineyard in Minervois, in the Languedoc region of southeastern France. This Grenache-based wine opens with an intriguing note of spicy smoke with an edge of watermelon and green apple and dashes of white pepper and orange zest. The fruit is balanced with a brisk acidity leading to a long finish with wraparound flavors. Terrific on its own or try with pasta in a light fish sauce or a mildly spiced pan-Asian dish.* * * *

Mas Karolina K Rosé

Mas Karolina is among the best of the new wave of Roussillon wines to appear in the last decade. Working with old vine Cinsault with a splash of Grenache Noir, Caroline Bonville has created an elegant rosé with lively minerality balanced against the vibrant red berry flavors of the Grenache. The minerality is a good example of impact of schist stones in the vineyard. This wine has the structure to match with pork, lamb or even a cassoulet.* * * * *

Domaine Lafage Miraflors

Priced at about $10, this is one of the best quality-for-value rosés to be found. Lafage is an historic estate in Roussillon with vineyards in the Agly Valley, near the wine village of Maury, and also near the Mediterranean, just north of the Spanish border. There's bright and eager fruit—strawberry and dried rose petals—and good acidity to make this a perfect match for a cookout around the grill or at the dinner table with a roast chicken.* * *

Prieuré Saint-Hippolyte

From vineyards in the heart of Languedoc, this fresh elbow bender from the co-op in the village of Fontés

opens on a fresh strawberry note with a dash of raspberries for added acidity. It's priced to be an everyday
wine, and we need all of those we can find. Match with
green salads, light cheese, olives, spiced nuts. . .get the
picture? * *

CHÂTEAU VIRANEL TRADITION

A zesty drink-me-now crowd pleaser from the
Saint-Chinian appellation in Languedoc. It is fresh and
bright on the nose, smelling of ripe red berries and a
touch of citrus. The flavors again focus on red berries
with an intriguing bitter edge. The finish is mouth filling and long. A good match with a variety of dishes,
including cold summer soups such as gazpacho or
mains like tagine with prunes, or paella.* * * *

Rest of France

CHÂTEAU D'AQUERIA

Generally regarded as the top estate in Tavel, with a
winemaking history going back to the 16th century,
this is Tavel rosé at the top of the game. It's a deep
salmon color with red fruit and garrigue at first sniff.
On the palate, the wine shows melon and strawberry
with a bracing minerality. There is abundant fruit and
a depth of flavor at the finish. It has the structure and

firmness to pair with a wide range of food, but it is especially delicious with shellfish.* * * * *

LES DAUPHINS

This pink wine from the southern Rhône Valley is sure to bring a smile to your face and a strong desire to reach for another glass. It's labeled as a Reserve but don't let that worry you. Les Dauphins made its reputation a century ago as a Bistro wine, happy to be invited to the party and sure to please. A blend of Grenache, Cinsault, and Syrah, it delivers a rich bouquet of fruit, especially white peach and lychee. The finish is bright and lively. A fine apéritif, but try it with a chicken on the grill or a selection of tapas.* * *

DYCKERHOFF PETIT GRIS

An elegant wine from the small and little known Reuilly AOC in the eastern part of the Loire Valley. The wines of Reuilly share a common limestone terroir with Sancerre and Chablis—wines of intense minerality. Based on Pinot Gris, the wine is balanced and supple, a crisp and refreshing apéritif with lingering lychee fruit notes. A five star selection, the wine shows best with lighter fare, such as a gazpacho-style cold melon soup.* * * * *

GUSTAVE LORENTZ LE ROSÉ

A remarkably full bodied Pinot Noir rosé from Alsace. It features delicious layers of fruit, principally red cherry and raspberry, matched with soft approachable tannins. The finish is long with echoes of the opening fruit plus a peppery age. An excellent apéritif but with the structure to go well with grilled pork as well as Asian cuisine.***

LUNAR APOGÉ

This biodynamic rosé from Tavel in the Rhône Valley is all about pleasure. The mouthfeel is supple and inviting, alive with cherry and red berry fruit, leading to a lingering finish with a spicy intensity. It is an elbow bender but with serious intentions. Serve it alone or with fresh fruit, young goat or sheep cheese, and good friends. More, please.***

DOMAINE MIOLANNE VOLCANE

From the Côtes d'Auvergane in the Loire Valley, this understated rosé offers a refreshing blend of Gamay and Pinot Noir fruit, elegant and lean. Named for a nearby dormant volcano. It is tempting to believe that the unusual soils, shaped by the ancient volcano, add to the restrained minerality of the wine. Match this with raw oysters, grilled fish, or a young cheese.***

LES ROMAINS

A classic Sancerre rosé of Pinot Noir from the Gitton family. Pale salmon in the glass, opening with light spice notes against a red fruit background. In the mid-palate the spice becomes more evident, a touch of cloves with a sniff of white pepper. It is fine as an apéritif, but it shines with food. Think of it as a Pinot Noir and match it with a "Pinot" dish. Especially good, too, with an aged Gouda cheese or chocolate truffles.****

DOMAINE DU TARIQUET ROSÉ DE PRESSÉE

A solid entry from Gascony, this blend of Merlot, Cabernet Franc, Syrah, and Tannat is a welcome *vin du plaisir*. It opens with firm fruit—raspberry and lemon—followed by a spicy finish with a touch of sage and thyme. Altogether, a wine to have on the table every day. Match this with a wide range of food, including grilled meats and aged cheese.**

PHILIPPE TESSIER CHEVRERNY

A fresh and delicious wine made from young vines on the Loire Valley estate vineyard. Tessier's stated goal is to make wine that "respects the natural balance" of the vines. The vineyard is organically farmed and only natural yeasts are used to start fermentation. The result is a very good wine, with a fine balance of minerality and red berry fruit with an edge of citrus. Try with raw oysters, grilled fish, or chicken.* * * * *

CHILL OUT

Rosé is often served too cold in the US, as is most white wine. On the other hand, red wines are often served too warm. Many wine guides suggest a temperature in the low 40s or even high 30s F. That does a great disservice to the wine. The colder the wine the lower the flavor profile. Cold mutes the fruit flavors of a wine, especially rosé, which at its best is a fairly delicate wine.

The problem often starts with the refrigerator. Most 'fridges are set for temperatures that are not wine friendly. How many people really know what the temperature is in their refrigerator? Let's see a show of hands, OK?

A good rosé, like you've been reading about in this guide, should be served in the low 50s F in order to show its full range of flavors. So the bottle should be taken out of the refrigerator at least 30 minutes before serving.

(continued)

If it still seems too warm, here's a little inside wine tip: put an ice cube in the glass before pouring the wine. Swirl the cube around in the glass for about a minute, then dump it. That will chill the glass enough to reduce the temperature of the wine. Here is an even more inside tip: it's OK to put an ice cube directly into the glass of wine for about the time it takes to count to ten, then remove it. It won't noticeably affect the taste of wine but will chill it a few degrees. You can do this with red wine, too, which is often served too warm, especially in restaurants.

If your guests sneer at you for putting a chill on it, just tell them Ann and Larry Walker said it was OK.

Ice-cold, stainless steel "whiskey stones"
work just as well in wine.

IBERIAN PENINSULA

ALANDRA

A youthful, inviting rosé from Portugal made from several native varieties with a tasty lashing of Syrah added for a firm, rounded structure. Clearly a starter wine (we need more of those) with lively red berry fruit, good acidity and spicy finish. Try with a tapa selection or pizza, extra anchovies please.* *

CASA FERREIRINHA VINHA GRANDE

Another outstanding rosé from the Broadbent Selections stable. Casa Ferreirinha was founded in 1751 and has been a global marketing giant for Portugal. This rosé from the Douro region of Portugal has intense red fruit aromas balanced with firm acidity and a long pleasing finish.* * *

CASAL GARCIA ROSÉ VINHO VERDE

An old favorite from Portugal. The wine is crisp and lively with engaging aromas and a bright finish. Makes a perfect apéritif but also a treat with spicy Southeast Asian dishes. And at only 10 percent alcohol, you can have a third glass. Who's counting? * * *

CASAL DE VENTOZELA

This rosado from Vinho Verde shows pale rose petal color in the glass, opening to bright, vivid fruit. It is made entirely from Espadeiro, an obscure Portuguese grape variety. The fruit—raspberry, strawberries with a touch of red cherry—is balanced by a firm acidity which lingers on the long finish. A very satisfying apéritif, the wine matches well with sausages, rice dishes—especially paella or risotto—and shellfish.* * *

DEFESA

A vivid and intense rosado from Esparao Estate vineyards in the Alentejo region of south Portugal. Based on Syrah and the ancient Iberian grape Argonez, it has lingering and well-rounded fruit tones with a penetrating minerality, reminiscent of wet stone. A good choice for dinner as it matches with grilled meats, pasta with tomato sauce, or as a starter with a chilled soup.* * * *

BODEGAS ESTABAN MARTIN BARON DE FUNES

A rosado from the Cariñena DO in northeastern Spain, a new hot spot for rosado, especially those made from Garnacha, which is becoming the go-to grape for pink wines in Spain. It opens with a youthful freshness on the palate, showing charming strawberry fruit. There is a pleasing minerality, which extends the finish, rounding out the fruit flavors. A true *vin du plaisir* apéro, also fine with simple grills. You could also throw a tapas party with plenty of this wine on hand.* * *

GAZELA

A charming rosé from the Vinho Verde region in Portugal, spicy cherry and raspberry aromas fairly leap from the glass. In the mouth there is a medley of red berry and ripe melon flavors. The finish is bright and merry, leaving anyone who takes immediate pleasure in a glass of wine reaching for another glass. Truly a drink-me-now elbow bender. More, please. Serve as an apéro or with olives, nuts, and young goat cheese.* *

LAGO CERQUEIRA

A hint of fizz on the opening following an intense opening nose of ripe strawberry and melon. There is good acidity balancing just a touch of sweetness that makes this rosé from Vinho Verde a perfect apéritif, perhaps with a bowl of olives or salted nuts. Altogether a light-hearted, friendly wine to hang out with.* *

JEAN LEON 3055 ROSÉ

An elegant Pinot Noir-based wine with vivid opening flavors of peach and citrus on a base of strawberry and red cherry. The wine has wraparound flavors that continue through the long finish. If you are wondering about the name—and why wouldn't you—3055 was the badge number of the taxi Jean Leon drove in New York City. Leon later opened La Sala restaurant in Hollywood and returned to Spain to establish Jean Leon Vineyards in Catalonia. The winery is now part of Torres Family Wines.* * * *

MATEUS ROSÉ

It hasn't lost its charm. For more than 75 years this Portuguese rosado has offered a deceptively simple solution to the question: where can I find a good, cheap, and reliable wine? This is it. It was 75 years ago and still is. It opens with intense aromas of crushed strawberries and melon, balanced on the palate with good acidity, restraining the closing sweetness. And the distinctive flask still makes a good candleholder.*

MATEUS EXPRESSIONS

This is the name of a new version of Mateus. It is not as sweet as the original and, alas, it doesn't come in a flask, but it does have the same opening intensity leading to a rounded finish. Take it on a picnic or have a bottle chilled the next time you order in Chinese or Indian food.*

MUGA

Without a doubt one of Spain's top rosés, from a leading producer of Rioja red wine. The Garnacha for the rosé is grown in a cooler site than the Garnacha for the red wine, which helps give a sharp and enticing minerality to the generous fruit. The color is pale orange with salmon tones. The opening flavors are citrus with a hint of green apple. The finish is long and layered, lingering and full on the palate. This is a rosé that could pair with what most consider red wine dishes. Grilled lamb comes happily to mind.*****

BODEGAS MURIEL

One taste of this rosado from Rioja and I was ready to jump on the next plane to Spain. It is, for sure, a Wow! kind of wine showing rich wraparound flavors, a delicious blend of Garnacha and Tempranillo. There is bright red cherry fruit on the opening leading to mid-flavors of strawberry backed by a firm minerality. It is easy drinking but also repays careful attention.

The finish is long with lingering fruit, including a hint of anise. This would match with grilled meats, pasta and rich stews. * * * * *

TOJEIRA

An appealing Vinho Verde rosé with red berry fruit, including a splash of cranberry. The mouthfeel is rounded with persistent fruit and minerality. There is brisk acidity in the finish, which is long and refreshing. The wine shines as an apéritif but also goes well with shellfish, grilled chicken and rice dishes. * *

TORRES DE CASTA ROSADO

A lively and delicious blend of Garnacha, Cariñena, Syrah and Tempranillo from the Torres home base in Viafranca del Penedés in Spain (Catalonia). The nose is intense, with orange and red cherry notes that run through the long finish. Miguel A. Torres began making this rosé in the 1940s, believing that wine drinkers deserved better than what was then available. The Torres family is still making it, and that's a very good thing. * * * * *

VIA LATINA

This Vinho Verde from the ancient Espadeiro grape is a bright, vivid rosado with pleasing strawberry aromas on the opening. There is intense and lingering raspberry fruit in the mouth, with a hint of spice and white pepper straight through to the long finish. At only 10 percent alcohol, it is a welcome apéritif at any hour of the day or time of the year. Also good with shellfish, grilled white fish or rice dishes such as paella.* * *

IN THE BEGINNING, THE WORD WAS MATEUS

There is a well-known photograph of the great guitarist Jimi Hendrix chugging Mateus rosé straight from the iconic flask shaped bottle. He was right on about what wine goes with rock music—rosé, of course—but Mateus is actually better drunk from a glass.

When the authors of this book were in college (age spoiler alert!), it was mandatory among the cool set to make empty Mateus bottles into candleholders. Who needs candleholders when there is Mateus? While researching this book, we discovered that our palate then was actually pretty good. Perhaps winemaking skills have improved, but the current version of Mateus is a very appealing wine (See Pink Choices, page 126).

It is arguable that the current trend to rosé can be dated back to 1942 when Fernando van Zeller Guedes, a winemaker

(continued)

from the Vinho Verde region of Portugal, was inspired by the slightly fizzy wines still common in Vinho Verde to produce a sweet and more full-bodied sparkling rosé for the world market. Guedes, who was the founder of the giant Sogrape wine conglomerate, the owners of Mateus, used the Douro red grape varietals, Baga, Rufete, Tinta Barroca and Touriga Franca, for the new wine. It turned out to be a very good idea. Mateus is not the force in the market that it was when Jimi Hendrix was knocking it back, but it is still going strong.

THE BEST OF THE REST OF THE PINK WORLD

BABYLONSTOREN FARM

A charming little rosé from the Western Cape region of South Africa. The wine, made from Mourvédre, is fairly simple, but sometimes simple is just what's needed in the glass. There's bright acidity and lively raspberry fruit, with a touch of strawberry and spice. Fetch another glass, please.* *

A.A. BADENHORST FAMILY WINES SECATEURS

A lively entry from South Africa, based on Cinsault and Syrah. Pale pink with opening strawberry and red cherry fruit. A pleasing apéritif but could also pair well with Asian or Mexican dishes as it has the fruit to deal with spice. In case you were wondering, *secateurs* is the French word for pruning shares, used to shape the vine and thus the wine.* * *

CORTE GARDONI

A rosé that is sure to bring a smile to your lips. Imported from the Veneto by Kermit Lynch, the Berkeley wine merchant who has done so much to help put rosé on the table, it is a blend based on Bardolino, called Chiaretto in Veneto. The wine is truly a pleasure to drink with bright cherry and strawberry dominating the opening and middle, held in check by a brisk minerality. The finish is long with a dash of light peppery spice. Serve with grilled lamb, pork or chicken or a garlicky pasta dish.* * *

CRIOS ROSÉ OF MALBEC

Owner and winemaker Susana Balbo makes exceptional wines, some of the best in Argentina, and she takes rosé seriously. It shows. There is deep fruit with a silky texture and a long finish. Don't rush this wine. Sip and savor. This is what good rosé is all about.* * * *

GEORGETOWN CENTRAL OTAGA ROSÉ OF PINOT NOIR

This wine proves that the New Zealand wine map goes way beyond Sauvignon Blanc. The grapes are from a single vineyard planted with closely-spaced vines, Burgundian style. The fruit is dominated by peaches, with a dash of ripe pear and a sprinkling of white pepper balanced with bright acidity. Good with cheese and cold cuts or grilled meats.* * * *

HUBER ZWEIGELT

An elegant rosé from Austria that, without making a big fuss, wraps itself seductively around the palate. It is a multi-layered wine, opening with penetrating aromas of strawberry and red cherry with hints of lime muted with just a wisp of honey. The center is creamy and rich leading to a wraparound finish, dry and long. An apéro, of course, but also try with a creamy blue cheese or a ripe cheddar style.* * * *

MULDERBOSCH

From South Africa's Coastal appellation, this rosé of Cabernet Sauvignon offers lush strawberry fruit tempered with intriguing floral aromas. The mid-palate is mouth filling with deep earthy flavors, rounded by typical brambly Cabernet fruit. The finish is long and satisfying with the strawberry fruit still dominant against a bright, acidic base.* * *

CUVÉE MUSAR

A rosé from the Cuvée line of wines produced by Château Musar, the famed Lebanese winery. An entire book could be (and probably has been) written about Musar, which was founded in 1930 and since then has missed only one vintage despite the years of conflict raging in Lebanon. The grapes—Cinsault and Mour-védre—are grown at a high altitude, which moderates the temperature. The vineyard is organically farmed. The wine is a pale pink color, very aromatic with intense fruit flavors on the opening, followed by hints of pomegranate and citrus. Slightly chilled, it makes an outstanding apéro but also matches quite well with grilled prawns, clam and fish stew or a plate or two of tapas.* * * * *

MIGUEL TORRES SANTA DIGNA

A bright and uplifted pink, with ripe fruit and mouth-filling flavors, very welcome as an apéro but quite willing to stand beside simple grills and pasta dishes. The winery was established in 1979 by Miguel Torres. The Spanish/Catalan winemaker realized the potential in Chile for sound but inexpensive wines and has been consistent in producing quality wines from a country not always known for high quality. This rosé of Cabernet Sauvignon is superb, an everyday table wine that never lets you down.* * *

VILLA GEMMA CERASUOLO D'ABRUZZO

A deeply colored rosado from the Masciarelli Italian wine house. The wine, from southern Italy, had a few hours more skin contact than most rosés, which has also added to the intensity of flavor. Tasted blind, in a black glass, this has some of the characteristics of a red wine from the Montepulciano grape. Some pink purists will object to this but it makes for a very bold rosé, and why not? The wine fills the palate with black fruit flavors—cherries and blackberries—with strong herbal aromas, mostly thyme and oregano. It makes a perfect pizza pink and would also work well with salami cold cuts and blue cheese.* * *

TORRE QUARTO INTRIGO

A slightly fizzy rosé from Puglia in southern Italy. The wine, made from a local grape called Uva di Troia, has a lively opening with a touch of red berries and cherries. The finish is rounded with a dash of white pepper adding taste texture. This worked well with an asparagus-based pasta dish.* *

WARWICK THE FIRST LADY

Made from Pinotage, South Africa's signature grape, this wine offers an intriguing minerality on the opening, balanced with brisk pomegranate and strawberry fruit. A good apéro but also matches well with grilled meats, especially pork.* *

A CASE OF QUALITY FOR VALUE

Rosé consistently delivers outstanding wine quality at very good value.

It is true that rosé price points are going up as consumers become more aware of how good the wine can be, but rosé is still a bargain. Here is a case-plus of good value rosé selected from Pink Choices. Prices are only approximate; they will vary depending on the store.

The average price for these 13 bottles of wine is a few cents over $13. Take that, wine snobs.

Check out detailed tasting notes in Pink Choices.

Dashe. A bright and fresh blend of Grenache and Zinfandel from the Dry Creek Valley. *$20*

Château Barbanau L'Instant. An everyday beauty that is the essence of a Provençal rosé. *$18*

Antech Emotion. An inviting bubbly from Limoux in the Languedoc. *$15*

Bokisch. A Garnacha-based rosé from Lodi in the San Francisco Bay Delta that is a ticket to Spain. *$15*

J. Lohr Gesture. This Grenache blend is a tribute to Rhône wines. *$14*

Domaine de Fontsainte Gris de Gris. An intense and refreshing rosé from Roussillon. *$14*

Domaine de Bila Haut. A delicious rosé from the up-and-coming Roussillon region of southeastern France. *$13*

Pedroncelli. A Zinfandel pink with deep roots in Sonoma County. *$12*

Torres de Casta. A spicy and delicious wine from the Torres family in Catalonia. *$12*

Gazela. A spicy and merry rosé from the Vinho Verde region of Portugal. *$10*

Château de Brigue. Your daily pink from Provence. *$10*

Domaine Lafage Miraflors. Outstanding quality for value from the Agly Valley in Languedoc. *$10*

Mulderbosch. This rosé of Cabernet Sauvignon from South Africa is an outstanding bargain. *$9*

DINING PINK

Part 1
Flavors

*T*here was a time that matching food and wine was simple: "red wine with meat, white wine with fish." That was the rule and no exceptions. Plenty of things are wrong with that, especially the matter of leaving rosé out of the equation.

The new rule could be: "when in doubt, bring the rosé out." Rosé can be matched with just about anything you put on the table.

Todd J. Smith, a certified sommelier and the wine director of two Indian restaurants in San Francisco said, "I love how versatile and diverse rosés can be."

When it comes to diversity, Smith has a full plate. The restaurants, both named Dosa, specialize in South

Indian cuisine, in which some dishes may contain 25–40 ingredients, according to Smith. "Some of our dishes can be wildly tropical, employing the ubiquitous coconut, mangoes, mountain spices, chilies, lentils, rice, rice, rice! Also, there are interior dishes that are smoky, earthy, woodsy and, certainly, spicy."

Smith likes to hunt for wines that can handle that kind of palate overload.

"Recently, I picked up a rosé of Milos Plavac Mali from Croatia. The winery has a 500-year history of wine-making so they know how to farm. This is a rosé that is so expressive, it can handle a wide variety of foods like no white or red. It is a wine that sings so well with bold cuisines," Smith said.

"Rosés are usually red fruited and pair so well with mint, tamarind, cumin, coriander, yogurt, black peppercorn, cloves, cinnamon, red lentils and the list goes on...," he said. Smith is so sold on rosé that he has a rosé made especially for Dosa's house wine.

"At the end of a night in which I help feed a few hundred people, it is time to sit down and dine. The first thing I do on most nights is pour a glass of rosé, set it upon the bar to mark my spot, then I go about to determine what I want for dinner," he said.

"I find that rosés pair with a greater swath of our menu than either white or red—in fact, it is the overlap of the three circles and so much fits inside," Smith said.

Smith is right, of course. While doing the tasting for this book, it became apparent that rosé is a more versatile wine with food than either red or white. Even though we were already big fans of pink wine, we were constantly surprised by how well the wines covered all bases. We realized that rosé is a chameleon. It has the ability to shape itself to the food on the plate, unlike, say, Cabernet Sauvignon or Chardonnay, which are locked into a fairly narrow flavor profile. Rosé—dry rosé, that is—has a much wider profile.

Why? It could be because rosé lacks the tannic structure of red or white wine and so is "softer" on the palate and more flexible.

We asked Oliver Brun, one of four brothers who own Château de Brigue in the heart of Provence, to help explain the food-friendly profile of rosé. The matching of wine with food is of special interest to the Brun family, as their estate produces its own olive oil, a key ingredient in Provençal cuisine.

"The range of food pairing with rosé is huge," he said. "For example, a lighter rosé with good fruit and acidity goes nicely with fish and white meats, such as chicken, while a stronger rosé with good structure makes a fine match with grilled red meat, such as lamb." Brun said that a more complex rosé, perhaps with a little oak aging, "is perfect with an old cheese."

"I believe that pairing with food is the great strength of Provence rosé," he concluded.

However, Brun believes that rosé, like red or white wine, is a product of terroir and does reflect the vineyard. "The quality comes first from the terroir. The grapes, too, are important. To me, the best grapes for rosé are Grenache, Mourvédre, and Cinsault. But the quality comes from the relationship between the vineyard and how the wine is fermented and developed. Terroir is the key." (See Pink Choices, page 108)

Part 2
Recipes, Well-Paired

The recipes we have developed for this book are designed to enhance the wine. That works both ways. The wine also enhances the food.

We have included a number of starters or tapas because rosé works so well with that kind of informal nibble. The main dishes do lean toward the fish/shellfish side of the menu. That is classic rosé territory. But there are a few meat dishes as well, showing the range that rosé can cover.

This brief selection of recipes is meant as a guide. Adjust them to your tastes and kitchen skills. They have all been double-tested and, for the most part, no special equipment is required. They are arranged in rough order from tapas and starters through main courses to desserts.

So, with a glass of rosé at hand, get ready to rattle those pots and pans.

STARTERS, TAPAS, MEZZE, SOUPS, SALADS & SAUCES

Green Olive Sauce

This easy-to-prepare sauce adds intense flavor and color to grilled fish or chicken.

Makes two cups

1 cup pimiento-stuffed olives, finely minced
2 garlic cloves, minced
2 tomatoes, seeded and cut into small dice
3 tablespoons olive oil
1 tablespoon sherry vinegar
salt and pepper to taste

Combine all ingredients and rest for two hours before using.

Mediterranean Plate

Serves six as a tapa

2 red bell peppers, roasted, peeled and cut or pulled
*   into strips*
4 eggs, hard boiled, cooled, quartered lengthwise
Anchovies packed in oil
Salt and pepper to taste
Olive oil

Note: Our favorite anchovies are from Cantabria and Collioure. Italian anchovies in olive oil and packed in jars are also readily available in the US.

Using long plates or a platter, alternate peppers, eggs, and anchovies. Sprinkle with a little salt and a grind of black pepper. Drizzle with a bit of extra virgin olive oil.

Fresh Fig and Anchovy Salad

Serves six

This summer salad, and a glass or two of pink wine, makes a perfect tapa.

1 large head curly endive, torn apart
12 fresh figs, stemmed
1 2-ounce can anchovies, drained and rinsed
3 ripe but firm medium tomatoes, peeled, seeded and
    cut into tiny dice
olive oil
black pepper

Divide the endive among six plates.

Cut figs into quarters and arrange in the center of the plates. Crisscross two fillets of anchovies over the figs and scatter the tomatoes over the entire dish.

Drizzle olive oil and sprinkle with pepper. Serve at once.

Crispy Shrimp Pancakes

Serves six to eight as a tapa

Note: Begin prep work about two hours in advance.

> *1 cup unbleached white flour*
> *1 cup garbanzo flour*
> *1 small bunch parsley, stemmed and minced*
> *1 medium onion, peeled and minced*
> *1 teaspoon salt*
> *½ teaspoon white pepper*
> *1 ½ cups water*
> *½ pound shrimp, peeled and coarsely chopped*
> *olive oil for frying*

Combine all ingredients except the oil in a bowl and let rest, covered, in the refrigerator for about two hours.

Heat about three tablespoons of olive oil in a large skillet to fry, but not deep fry.

Drop the batter by the spoonful into the oil to form three to four inch cakes. Cook until golden on both sides and drain on paper towels.

Serve at once. The pancakes should be eaten while they are still hot and the edges crisp.

Skillet Mussels with Green Sauce

Serves four to six

3 dozen black mussels, cleaned and debearded

Sauce:

1 poblano chili	*½ cup olive oil*
½ cup cilantro	*2 tablespoons white*
1 serrano chili	*balsamic vinegar*
½ teaspoon salt	

Rinse the shells and debeard the mussels. Set aside.

Meanwhile: Roast the poblano chili over a flame or under a broiler. Remove and put in a bag or bowl, covered. When cool enough to handle, remove the stem and seeds. Peel the chili.

In a blender or food processor, grind the poblano, cilantro, chili, salt, oil, and vinegar. Thin with a little water if necessary.

Heat a heavy cast iron skillet over high heat. When very hot, add the mussels all at once. Sprinkle with 2 tablespoons of water. Shake the skillet and stir the mussels until they pop open. Pour the sauce over the mussels and serve from the skillet.

Prawns with Garlic

Serves six as a tapa

> *3 tablespoons olive oil*
> *18 medium sized prawns, shelled and deveined*
> *½ teaspoon salt*
> *5 garlic cloves, peeled and thinly sliced*
> *½ teaspoons smoked hot Spanish paprika*
> *½ cup dry white wine*
> *1 tablespoon cold butter*
> *1 tablespoon finely minced parsley*

Heat the oil in a medium skillet. When the oil is very hot, add the prawns and sprinkle with salt. Toss in the oil for one minute.

Add the garlic and paprika and cook until the prawns are pink. Pour in the wine and cook briskly over a high flame for another minute while the sauce thickens.

Stir in a tablespoon of cold butter and shake and swirl the skillet.

Sprinkle with parsley and serve straight from the skillet with lots of crusty bread for dipping into the sauce.

Calamari Salad

Serves ten as a tapa

10 cloves garlic
¾ cups chopped parsley
¾ cup basil
½ teaspoon dried thyme
*   leaves*
2 ounces anchovy fillets
½ teaspoon each salt
*   and black pepper*
½ cup olive oil
½ cup red wine vinegar
juice of 2 lemons

1 pound cleaned squid
*   tubes and tentacles*
1 each medium red and
*   green bell pepper,*
*   stemmed, seeded*
*   and cut into thin*
*   strips*
1 medium red onion,
*   peeled and sliced*
*   into thin rings*

In a food processor or blender, grind together the garlic, parsley, cilantro, cumin, anchovies, salt, and pepper. In a small bowl, combine the oil, vinegar, and lemon juice. With the motor running, slowly add to the ground mixture. Set this dressing aside in a bowl.

Bring a large pot of salted water to a boil. Cut the squid tubes into ¼ inch rings, leaving the tentacles whole. Blanch the squid in the boiling water for about 30 seconds. Remove and toss the cooked squid with the dressing. Fold in the peppers and onions. Refrigerate overnight before serving.

Ginger Pickled Salmon With Wasabi Crème Fraiche

Note: Begin prep of the salmon 4 days before serving.

Ten to twenty cocktail servings

This recipe looks intimidating, but is fairly simple when broken down into steps and is always a crowd pleaser.

GINGER PICKLED SALMON

Day 1

> *1 pound skinless fillet of salmon, cut into 1-inch cubes*
> *3 ½ teaspoons salt*

Sprinkle a 9 × 13" non-reactive container with 1½ teaspoons salt. Put the salmon on the salt and sprinkle with the remaining salt. Cover and refrigerate overnight. The next day, rinse off the salt and pat dry.

Combine and bring to a boil:

> *1cup water*
> *1 cup white wine vinegar*
> *2 tablespoons brown sugar*

Day 2

Mix:

>1 teaspoon coriander seeds
>1 teaspoon yellow mustard seed
>1 tablespoon pickling spices
>1/4 teaspoon hot red pepper flakes

In a separate bowl mix 1 medium onion, halved and sliced, with ¼ cup peeled and thinly sliced ginger.

Mix the salmon with the onion and ginger. Sprinkle the spices over each layer. Pour the vinegar mixture over the salmon. Cover and refrigerate at least 2 days. Toss the salmon each day.

THE CRÈME FRAÎCHE

Day 1

Combine in a glass jar 1 cup heavy cream with 1 table-spoon sour cream.

Cover the jar and put in a warm place for the cream to thicken. This can take 1 to 3 days depending on the temperature.

Just before serving:

Combine 2 teaspoons wasabi powder with 2 teaspoons water. Stir until a smooth paste is formed and stir the wasabi into the crème fraîche.

To Serve

Method 1—for the appetizer table

Arrange the salmon on a platter and serve the crème fraîche in a separate bowl as a dip.

Method 2—for a tray passed appetizer

Cut the chunks of salmon in half and serve the salmon on corn pancakes or on rye toasts topped with a dab of the crème fraîche.

Note: The salmon will keep refrigerated for 2 weeks.

The crème fraîche is good for one week. You may also substitute fresh Mexican crema for the crème fraîche.

A COOKIE AND A GLASS OF ROSÉ

There is a small bakery/café in our San Francisco neighborhood where we sometimes make a stop during a walkabout. We always have a glass of rosé each and share an oversized chocolate chip cookie. Well, sometimes two glasses of rosé but never more than one cookie. Mostly.

When you think about it, a cookie and a rosé seem to be a perfect match. That's the great thing about rosé. It can be a mid-afternoon indulgence while reading a few pages or quietly people watching in a small café. Not just any rosé, mind you. It has to be a serious rosé that doesn't take itself too seriously. A rosé with a light touch yet lingering on the palate.

Our choice is often the Broadbent Vinho Verde. Portugal, of course. It is an elegant wine with bright and intense fruit that dances in your mouth. Finishes clean and bright with that pleasing hint of fizz that is typically Vinho Verde.

It is imported by Broadbent Selections. You will have to source your own cookie.

MAIN DISHES

Carrot Soup, with an Asian Touch

Serves four to six

This is a recipe you can play with. It works as a starter, or could be the main soup for a light lunch.

> *1 medium onion*
> *½ cup thinly sliced and peeled ginger coins*
> *6 large carrots, cut into ½-inch rounds*
> *1 teaspoon salt*
> *½ teaspoon pepper*

Peel and chop the onion into 3 tablespoons of butter. Sauté until limp. Add ginger and cook until fragrant. Add to the onion mixture. Bring to a boil, cover, and reduce heat. Cook until the carrots are soft. Pour everything into a blender or, even better, a Vitamix.

Blend, starting at the lowest speed and gradually increasing to high, and continue blending until very smooth. Add water to achieve the consistency you want. Taste, and add salt and pepper as needed. You could also add plain yogurt or cream. Maybe some orange zest. Make it your own.

Gazpacho

Serves four

This variation on a Spanish classic plays with the zesty flavor of fresh tomato on the finish.

> 2 tablespoons olive oil
> 1 large onion, minced
> ½ celery stalk, thinly sliced
> 3 tomatoes
> 3 cups chicken stock
> 1 bay leaf
> 2 cloves
> 1 cup ½-inch day-old bread cubes

Heat the oil and slowly cook the onion and celery until very tender but not yet colored.

Purée two of the tomatoes and stir into the onions. Cook quickly until the tomatoes form a paste. Pour in the stock and add the bay leaf, cloves, salt, and pepper to taste.

Cook for 30 minutes over low heat. Peel, seed, and cube the remaining tomato. Add to the soup just before serving and heat through. Stir in the breadcrumbs and serve.

Roasted Garlic and Blue Cheese Mousse

Serves eight to ten

20 large cloves of garlic, peeled
8 ounces mascarpone
8 ounces blue cheese

Preheat oven to 400°F.

Wrap the garlic in foil and roast 30 minutes or until soft. Unwrap and let cool.

Beat the mascarpone and blue cheese together in a mixer or food processor. Add garlic and purée until smooth.

Have a small bowl ready lined with dampened cheesecloth. Pour the mixture into bowl, pull the cheesecloth up to cover the top. Refrigerate overnight.

Fold back the cheesecloth from the top of the mousse, place a plate on top and invert. Gently peel the cheesecloth off the mousse.

Surround the mousse with endive spears. The mousse is delicious eaten on the spears. Serve more endive spears, crostini or crackers on the side.

Eggplant Salad

Serves six

This works as stand-alone tapa, as a main course, or as a side dish with grilled meat or fish.

> *¼ cup olive oil or more as needed*
> *2 pounds eggplant, unpeeled and cut into ½-inch dice*
> *1 medium onion, chopped*
> *2 red or green bell peppers, seeded, cut into ½-inch dice*
> *3 tomatoes, peeled and chopped*
> *¼ cup sugar*
> *2 tablespoons red wine vinegar*
> *2 tablespoons capers*

Heat the oil in a large skillet. When very hot, add eggplant and toss to coat with the oil. Lower heat to medium. Sprinkle lightly with salt and pepper. Cook until the eggplant begins to color. Remove and drain on paper towels.

Add more olive oil to the skillet if necessary and cook onions and pepper until soft. Stir in the tomatoes and cook until most of the liquid has evaporated. Return eggplant to the skillet, stir in the sugar, vinegar, and capers. Cook over low heat until the eggplant is soft but still holds its shape. Season with additional salt and pepper if needed.

Serve hot or at room temperature, as the flavor will improve as the dish cools. If refrigerated, let warm to room temperature before serving.

Clams in Green Sauce

Serves six as a first course or ten as a tapa

2 pounds manila clams
   in their shells
1 cup dry white wine
2 tablespoons olive oil
6 garlic cloves, minced
¼ cup minced onion

¼ cup minced parsley
1 teaspoon all-purpose
   flour
Salt and freshly ground
   black pepper to taste

Clean the clams. Bring the wine to a boil in a saucepan and add clams. Steam clams and remove from the pan as soon as they open. Discard any that do not open. Remove and discard the top shell of the clams, leaving meat attached to the bottom shell. Set clams aside.

Reduce the liquid to 1 cup.

Heat the oil in a skillet and cook the garlic and onion until soft. Stir in the parsley and cook one minute with the flour. Strain the reduced steaming liquid into the skillet to remove any grit. Cook until the sauce begins to thicken. Season with salt and pepper, if needed. The clams are pretty salty.

Add clams to the sauce and simmer for 5 minutes.

Serve on plates or in a clay casserole for all to share, with lots of good crusty bread for dipping in the sauce.

Monkfish in Brandy Cream Sauce

Serves six to eight

> *2 pounds monkfish fillets*
> *2 tablespoons olive oil*
> *1/3 cup minced shallots*
> *salt and white pepper to taste*
> *¼ cup brandy*
> *1 tablespoon tomato paste*
> *½ cup cream*
> *¼ cup finely minced parsley*

Remove and discard skin from monkfish fillets and cut the fish crossways into 1-inch thick medallions.

Heat the oil in a large skillet and cook the shallots slowly until tender. Place the fish in the pan and sprinkle with salt and white pepper. Cook for one minute on each side.

Pour in the brandy, wait a few seconds for the fumes to settle, and carefully ignite. Combine and stir in the tomato paste and cream. Raise the heat and cook until the sauce thickens and the fish is cooked.

Serve immediately, sprinkled with fresh parsley.

Rockfish and Clams in Black Bean-Garlic-Ginger Cream

Note: Do not add salt or pepper when cooking this dish. There is enough from the clam liquid and the bean paste.

Serves four

> 20 *littleneck clams, shells washed clean*
> ½ *cup dry white vermouth*
> 20 *oz. rockfish fillets, bones removed and cut into*
>   *serving portions*
> 2 *tablespoons vegetable oil*
> ¾ *cup yellow onion, minced*
> 2 *tablespoons ginger, peeled and minced*
> ¼ *cup cream*
> 1 *heaping tablespoon Chinese black bean-garlic paste*

Heat the vermouth in a lidded pan large enough to hold all the clams. Add the clams, cover, and cook over medium heat, shaking the pan a couple of times until all the clams are open. Pour the clams through a sieve over a bowl to catch the cooking liquid. Set the clams aside.

Warm the soup plates in a low oven.

Heat the oil in a lidded skillet large enough to hold all the fish. Cooking time will depend on how crowded the pan is. Take this into consideration.

Cook the onions and ginger over medium-low heat until the onions begin to brown. Add the fish, cover, and cook for 3 minutes.

Turn the fish over and cook, covered, for another 3 minutes or until the fish is cooked through and still holding its shape. Remove the fish and divide among the 4 serving plates.

Pour the clam liquid into the onion mixture and increase the heat. Boil. Add the cream and bean paste. The mixture will bubble up. Stir and then let reduce until the thickness of a light cream.

Meanwhile, surround the fish with the clams in their shells. Pour the sauce over the fish and clams. Serve immediately with rice or crusty breads.

Rockfish in Apple Cider Vinegar

Serves 6

3 tablespoons shallots, finely minced

3 small tomatoes, peeled, seeded and puréed

¼ cup organic, unfiltered apple cider vinegar

½ cup white wine

1 cup fish stock or bottled clam juice

2 ½ pounds of rockfish fillets cut into 6 serving portions

salt and pepper to taste

¼ cup cream

2 tablespoons capers, drained

Combine the shallots, tomatoes, vinegar, and wine in a large non-reactive skillet. Cook over medium heat until most of the liquid has evaporated. Stir in the fish stock and bring to a boil. Lower the heat and add the fish. Sprinkle with salt and pepper. If you've used bottled clam juice, be careful how much salt you add. Gently poach the fish in the liquid until firm, about seven minutes, depending on the thickness of the fillets. Remove to a platter and keep warm.

Add the cream to the skillet and boil to thicken. The sauce should be as thick as heavy cream. Stir in the capers. Taste for seasoning, adding more salt or pepper if needed. Pour the sauce over the fish and serve immediately.

Sausage and Beans with Allioli

Serves six to eight

About as basic as you can get. It can certainly be enjoyed without the allioli, but the Spanish sauce does add a certain pop to the dish.

The Sausages

> *6 ½ pounds mild Italian-style sausages*
> *2 tablespoons olive oil*
> *6 cups white beans, cooked and partially drained*
> *salt and pepper to taste*
> *2 tablespoons finely minced parsley*
> *1 cup allioli*

Prick the sausages in several places and grill or pan fry until done. Meanwhile, heat the oil and sauté the beans, seasoning with salt and pepper.

To serve, divide the beans among six plates and put a sausage on the side and a dollop of allioli on top. Sprinkle with the parsley.

The Allioli

Makes two cups

> *4 or 5 medium sized garlic cloves, peeled*
> *2 egg yolks*
> *1 ½ cups olive oil*
> *salt to taste*

This is best made using a mortar and pestle. Crush the garlic until a rough paste is formed. Stir in the egg yolks, using the pestle. Always stir in the same direction so the surface tension of the mixture is not broken. Continue stirring while very slowly adding the oil until a thick crush is formed. Sprinkle in salt to taste. The allioli should be slightly stiff—you should be able to stand a spoon upright in the sauce.

This can also be made in a blender if you want to cheat. Simply put the garlic, the egg yolk, and one whole egg in a blender. Slowly add the oil with the blender running until the mixture is about the consistency of mayonnaise.

Paella Weber-Style

Paella and pink wine are a perfect match, and how better to bring them together than in the garden. After all, in Spain, paella purists insist that the dish should be made over an open fire using vine trimmings. Of course, if you are having a rainy day paella, this dish can easily be prepared indoors at the kitchen stove.

Serves six from a 9-inch paella pan

3 tablespoons olive oil
1 medium onion, minced
3 garlic cloves, minced
1 pound tomatoes, chopped
1 ½ pounds boneless chicken thighs, cut into medium sized chunks
½ pound squid tubes, cut into ¼-inch slices
¼ pound Spanish chorizo, cut into ¼-inch slices
2 teaspoons salt, or more to taste
6 cups very hot chicken stock
½ teaspoon saffron threads
3 cups short grain rice
1 pound mussels in shells or a combination of mussels and clams
1 pound prawns in shells
1 cup fresh peas or 1 pound asparagus tips (optional)
Lemon slices

Light the coals in a Weber-type, round-lidded barbecue. Place the paella pan on the grill above the hot coals and pour in the oil. When hot, add the onion and garlic and cook until limp.

Stir in the tomatoes and cook until dry.

Move the vegetables to the side of the pan. Add the chicken, squid, and chorizo. Sprinkle with salt.

Rub the saffron threads between your palms and sprinkle into the hot broth.

Cook, turning the chicken over until it begins to color, about five minutes, depending on the heat under the pan. Add the stock or water.

At this time you may need to stoke the fire to bring the stock to a boil. Taste for salt. The broth should taste slightly salty. Cook at a rapid boil for about five minutes.

Stir in the rice, turning the chicken pieces over so the rice is submerged in the broth, and cook for about ten minutes.

Arrange the prawns over the top of the paella.

Add the mussels hinge-side down around the edge. Cook for another five minutes, covered.

Add the peas or asparagus now. Close the cover and cook for another five minutes.

Test a piece of rice. It should be a little firm to the teeth. If not, cook a bit longer, covered.

To serve, take the paella to the table and cover with a cloth and let rest for about 5 minutes. Then decorate the top of the paella with lemon wedges. Garnish each serving with a lemon wedge so your guests can squeeze the lemon juice over the paella.

Just the Best Roast Chicken

Mix and keep in an airtight container

1 cup garlic powder
1 cup dried oregano
1 tablespoon turmeric
salt to taste

Rub some of this mixture onto chicken pieces. Cover and refrigerate overnight.

Sprinkle the chicken pieces with a little salt and roast in a preheated 450°F oven for about 30 minutes or until done.

Reserve the rest of the rub for later.

EVEN PORT IS TURNING PINK

In an attempt to catch the rosé sales trend, usually deeply traditional producers of Port wines are now making Pink Port. The rules governing Port production are complex, depending on the style of Port. Pink Port doesn't exactly break any of the rules but carves out its own niche in the Ruby Port category. Ruby is the most commonly produced Port. It is based on red grapes, of course, and aged only briefly compared to Tawny or Vintage Ports. Rosé Port begins life as a Ruby but is quickly taken off the skins, creating a pale pink wine, as in traditional rosé production.

The first Port House to make a rosé was Taylor-Fladgate, which has introduced a rosé under their Croft label. According to market reports, the wine is selling very well, especially in restaurants and bars. Some bartenders, pushing the Port parameters even more, are using a slushy machine to make icy drinks, a kind of popsicle Port for adults.

SWEET ENDINGS

Rosé Braised Apricots with Crunchy Almonds

My favorite apricots are the ones with the slight pink blush which, of course, makes me think of rosé wine.

Try this recipe when you have some special apricots available.

1 ½ cups of rosé wine
¼ cups granulated sugar
1 sprig of fresh thyme
6 small, not too ripe apricots

4 tablespoons creme fraiche

½ cup whole almonds, chopped, plus ¼ cups granulated sugar

Pour the wine into a non-reactive skillet and stir in the sugar and sprig of thyme. Warm over a medium heat until the sugar has melted.

Cut the apricots in half and place cut side down in the wine. Cover the pan and cook gently until the apricots soften a bit but still hold their shape. Watch carefully.

Using a slotted spoon, remove the apricots to a plate. Remove the sprig of thyme and discard. Increase the heat and reduce the cooking liquid until med-thick syrup consistency. Remove from the heat.

Meanwhile caramelize the almonds. Pour the ¼ cup sugar into a medium hot, smallish heavy skillet and when the sugar begins to melt around the edges, add the almonds. Cook over the medium heat, stirring the almonds while the sugar continues to caramelize. Cook the almonds until darkish, golden brown. Pour the almonds out onto a buttered sheet pan. Let cool completely. Chop the almonds finer. You may not want to use all the almonds with the apricots but any left over almonds will, no doubt, find a place in your salads.

Arrange the apricots on a platter or individual dessert plates, three halves for a serving. Place a spoonful of creme fraiche on the plate.

Drizzle the apricots with the syrup and just before serving, sprinkle them with the crushed caramelized almonds.

Tarta de Musico (Musicians' Tart)

This tart is a modern adaptation of a very simple Catalan dessert based on the tradition of giving dried fruits and nuts to traveling musicians. Traditionally served with a glass or porron of muscatel. Try this with a glass of sparkling rosé!

Serves eight

Pastry

1 ½ cups flour

2 tablespoons sugar

½ cup unsalted butter,
 cut into pieces

1 egg, separated

3 tablespoons ice water

Filling

1 cup sugar

½ cup unsalted butter

½ cup whipping cream

½ cup pine nuts

¼ cup sliced almonds

¼ cup dried mission figs,
 diced raisin size

¼ cup pitted prunes,
 diced raisin size

½ cup raisins

1 tablespoon brandy

1 teaspoon almond
 extract

The Pastry

Combine flour and sugar in a food processor.

With the motor running, cut the butter into the flour with a few pulses.

Add the egg yolk and mix quickly.

Add the water, one tablespoon at a time, pulsing, until the mixture holds together.

Turn the pastry out onto a flat surface and form into a ball. Flatten into a round to fit a 9-inch tart pan with removable rim. Turn the edges under to form a double rim. Refrigerate for 30 minutes.

Preheat the oven to 350°F.

Line the tart shell with waxed paper and fill with dried beans or pie weights. Bake for 15 minutes.

Remove the paper and the beans or weights.

Beat the remaining egg white and brush the crust, then bake for 10 minutes more.

Remove from the oven and set aside.

Raise the heat to 375°F.

THE FILLING

Cook the sugar and butter in a heavy bottomed pan, stirring until the sugar dissolves and begins to caramelize. Cook to a dark golden color.

Pour in the cream and mix well.

Stir in the nuts, fruits, brandy, and almond extract, and remove from heat.

Pour into the tart shell and smooth the top.

Place in the oven and bake for 20 minutes.

Remove from the oven and allow the tart to rest until firm, about two hours. Remove the rim and serve.

AFTERWORD

HOW ROSÉ SAVED OUR VILLAGE

*I*t was an idle conversation over a bottle of Roussillon rosé and a plate of assorted olives on the terrace of our home in the French village of Maury. Why are some villages vital, alive, fun to hang out in, while others seem to be dying, little more than dusty and often dreary remains of centuries past with little promise of a future? There are villages nearby as large or larger than Maury that have no café, no shops of any kind, no center in a cultural or commercial sense. One might as well be living in a suburban housing development somewhere in deepest Oklahoma. Once we were driving though a village only a few kilometers from Maury when Ann developed a sudden thirst. We spotted three men talking in a small plaza. Ann pulled over and we asked if there was a café in town. The older of the three men smiled and said, "We are the café."

Maury is something of a border town. Border cities often tend to be lively places, culture clash and all that. If you dip back into a thousand years-plus of history, the ancient border between Catalan speakers to the east and Occitan speakers to the west was the Agly River. Estagel, the next town to the west down the D117 is on the east side of the Agly and is traditionally Catalan speaking. In the Middle Ages, there were frequent skirmishes between the two groups, and there are still reports of teenagers (perhaps with a keen historical sense) staging cross-border raids.

I poured another glass of rosé all around. We agreed that the historical line of thought was interesting but didn't explain why Maury is more "there" than most villages around and about.

"I think it's this mayor of yours," said Tim, a visitor from London and an old BBC hand, given to quick journalistic analysis.

The mayor at that time was Charles Chivilo, a man determined to put Maury on the touristic map. Chivilo was a guiding force behind Maison du Terroir, the home of a star restaurant, as well as wine tasting and a sales room for local artisan products. He has promoted music festivals and exhibits to attract visitors to Maury. His promotional activities have not always set well with the locals, yet I think it would be difficult to argue with the flow of euros.

Julie, a friend from New Orleans, is a novelist, so she is always looking for plot twists. "I think it's the wine."

She held out her empty glass. "More pink wine, please."

INDEX OF PRODUCERS

Index of Producers

INDEX OF WINES

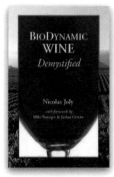

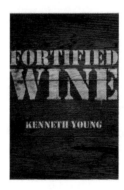